本书获上海外国语大学科研项目基金出版资助

外语课堂教学中的否定反馈
Negative Feedback in EFL Classrooms

胡越竹 著

世界图书出版公司

上海·西安·北京·广州

图书在版编目(CIP)数据

外语课堂教学中的否定反馈:英文/胡越竹著.—上海:上海世界图书出版公司,2013.6
ISBN 978-7-5100-5609-3

Ⅰ.①外… Ⅱ.①胡… Ⅲ.①英语—口语—课堂教学—教学研究—英文 Ⅳ.①H319.9

中国版本图书馆 CIP 数据核字(2013)第 006801 号

责任编辑:应长天
装帧设计:车皓楠
责任校对:石佳达

外语课堂教学中的否定反馈

胡越竹　著

上海世界图书出版公司 出版发行
上海市广中路 88 号
邮政编码 200083
上海市印刷七厂有限公司印刷
如发现印装质量问题,请与印刷厂联系
(质检科电话:021-59110729)
各地新华书店经销

开本:890×1240　1/32　印张:5.5　字数:380 000
2013 年 6 月第 1 版　2013 年 6 月第 1 次印刷
ISBN 978-7-5100-5609-3/H·1239
定价:30.00 元

http://www.wpcsh.com.cn
http://www.wpcsh.com

序　言

　　外语学习过程中不可避免会出现各类语言错误,这些错误的存在给学习者造成了很大的困扰,尤其是内向、自信心弱、学习水平较低的学生。作为一名具有高度责任感的外语教师,作者最初关注否定反馈问题就是源于对这一点的认识。在大量阅读国内外学术期刊相关文章的基础上,作者曾进行小范围的实证研究,并在国内核心期刊上发表了研究结果。而本书在作者的博士论文基础上修订而成的,内容涉及面更广、更深入,研究设计更新、更全面,统计数据分析更透彻,具有创新性,对改进外语教学具有很好的指导作用。

　　本书具有以下特点:

　　1. 内容丰富

　　作者在阅读大量相关资料的基础上对现有文献中错误的定义、分类、成因、评定标准以及否定反馈的必要性、作用和决定因素等问题进行了深入分析,根据二语习得理论提出了更合理的想法,接着对作者的研究对象、方法、数据搜集和分析结果进行了详细阐述,本书科学运用了注意假设、语言发展阶段假设、输入说、输出说、技能习得等二语习得理论对语言学习的各种现象和过程进行了剖析,同时运用了认知心理学、社会心理学、人格心理学和教育心理学分析学生的需求和个体差异,探讨否定反馈的实用性和适用性问题。

　　2. 视角独特

　　笔者通过大范围的实证研究,对于外语学习环境中教师提供否定反馈的情况进行了深入系统的调查分析,详细对比了教师的纠错行为与学生需求的差异,这在二语习得领域尚属首次。还有一些外语课堂教学中被忽略的重要问题,如小组活动中的同伴反馈问题、学习者的学习水平、性格、自信心强弱、第二课堂焦虑感强弱等在否定反馈方面的不同需求等问题,在本书中也进行了详细分析和讨论。

3. 指导实践

本书作者对于错误和否定反馈相关问题的想法能够帮助学者们运用新视角、从不同的角度看问题,有利于拓宽视野、增进认识。而本次实证研究的独特设计,尤其是第二语言自信心、第二语言焦虑感、冒险性等个体差异问题与否定反馈相关性的研究,将给学者们以新的启示,激发其研究兴趣,有利于促进二语习得研究,尤其是学习者心理研究的发展。就研究结果而言,本书的详细分析有利于教师了解学生的学习心理和不同需求、了解同伴反馈情况、发现教学中的不足之处,从而改善教学,调整和丰富教学手段和方法,使学生从外语课堂的否定反馈中最大程度受益。这对于实现高等学校的教学目标、培养高水平的复合型外语人才有积极作用。

希望本书的出版能增进外语教学研究者和工作者对否定反馈和语言学习过程的认识,进一步促进我国的外语教学。

2013 年 5 月 30 日

摘　　要

外语学习过程中,由于学习者缺乏语言知识或缺少可以随时正确运用的程序化知识,语言错误不可避免。过去行为主义学派认为,外语学习就是形成新的语言习惯,而错误被看做失败的标志,逢错必究。随着认知主义理论的发展和人们对语言学习过程的了解不断深入,语言错误不再被看做洪水猛兽,而成为促进语言学习的工具。研究表明,只提供肯定反馈会导致一些错误的语言形式长时间存在于中介语中,产生石化,致使学习者到达某一发展阶段后无法进一步提高。事实上,纠正语言错误不仅必需,而且有很大的促进作用。它能帮助学习者进行认知对比、调整假设、加速语言规则和知识的吸收。对于我国的大学生来说,课堂教学是学习和提高语言能力的主要途径,教师的课堂纠错行为对学生中介语的形成和发展有重要影响。然而,就目前情况来看,否定反馈方面的研究多集中于外语学习者与本国语者的对话和沉浸式教学,虽然有学者已开始进行英语作为外语(EFL)的课堂教学调查,但对于教师在外语课堂的纠错行为、学生在小组活动中的同伴反馈和学生个体差异我们知之甚少。本书作者旨在通过实证研究,对外语环境中课堂否定反馈情况进行深入了解和分析,以求找到更有效的教学方法提高教学水平,改善外语教学。

本书共分为五章。

第一章简要介绍了写作背景、写作目的和篇章结构。

第二章详细阐述了以往否定反馈研究中语言错误的定义、类型、成因、评定标准以及人们对待语言错误的态度和错误严重性的评估标准。总体而言,语言错误可根据三方面进行判断:形式是否正确、上下文是否合适以及是否有可接受性。母语干扰、语内迁移、误导性教学和交际技巧的运用等原因会导致语言能力错误出现，而语言使用错误的出现可能由于学习者认知和心理方面的局限所致。

第三章是关于否定反馈问题，分为四节，即否定反馈的定义、必要性和作用、决定因素以及研究综述。否定反馈也称为"否定输入"、"纠正性反馈"、"反馈"，给予否定反馈时应考虑多方面因素，如活动的目标、与标准语的偏离度、语义清晰度、出现频率、学习者语言水平、情感因素、性格因素等。现有的文献可从错误反馈频率、反馈错误类型、反馈方式、反馈时间和反馈者等五方面进行分析。

第四章阐述了本次实证研究的目的、方法、结果，就反馈频率、纠错类型、反馈方式等问题进行讨论。研究对象包括五所大学352名一年级学生和十二所大学80位外语教师，研究结果如下：

1. 教师的纠错频率不高，纠正最多的是表达错误，其次是语法错误和语音错误。教师采用最多的纠错方式是重述和启发。有部分教师使用非语言方式提供否定反馈。大多数情况下教师在学生结束表达后提供反馈。全班性课堂活动和小组讨论及两人活动时教师的纠错行为有所不同。

2. 英专教师和非英专教师纠错行为的不同之处表现在：1）英专教师的纠错频率较非英专教师低；2）相对而言，英专教师纠正学生的表达错误更多，而非英专教师纠正语法错误和语音错误更多；3）英专教师更常采用要求说明的纠错方式，而非英专教师更常采用明确纠正和元语言反馈。

3. 大多数教师在纠错时考虑到了学生个体差异。对于低水平学生、女同学、缺乏自信心的学生、冒险性差的学生和焦虑感强的学生教师的纠错频率相对较低。对于内向和外向学生、较高水平的学生和较低水平的学生、自信心强和自信心弱的学生、冒险性强和冒险性弱的学生以及焦虑感强和焦虑感弱的学生教师采取的纠错方式有所不同。

4. 学生对语言错误和教师纠错持肯定态度,但不希望教师过于频繁地纠错。他们认为最有必要得到纠正的是语音错误和表达错误,希望教师提供机会给他们自己纠正错误,特别是英专学生。大多数学生希望教师在他们表达结束后纠正错误。他们赞成教师在全班性课堂活动和小组活动或两人活动时采用不同的纠错方式。总的来说,教师的纠错行为符合学生的要求。

5. 较高水平的学生、自信心强的学生、冒险性强的学生和第二语言信心强的学生希望教师采用能让他们自纠的纠错方式。较低水平的学生、冒险性弱的学生和焦虑感强的学生和第二语言信心弱的学生最喜欢的纠错方式是重述。

6. 学生对于同伴纠错持肯定态度。他们在小组讨论和两人活动时不常相互纠错。他们纠正同伴最多的是语音错误,最常采用的同伴纠错方式是重述。

7. 较高水平的学生、外向学生、自信心强的学生、冒险性强的学生、焦虑感弱的学生和第二语言信心强的学生更常提供机会让同伴自己纠错。较低水平的学生和自信心弱的学生常采用重述纠正同伴的错误。冒险性弱的学生和第二语言自信心弱的学生喜欢明确纠正同伴的错误。

8. 相对于低水平学生、内向学生和冒险性弱的学生而言,高水平学生、外向学生和冒险性强的学生更喜欢能让他们自纠的同伴纠错方式。焦虑感强的学生最喜欢重述的纠错方式,焦虑感弱的学生最喜欢明确纠正。第二语言信心弱的学生喜欢明确纠正,第二语言信心强的学生喜欢重述。

本书第五章再次总结了研究结果,进一步阐述了该研究对于改进外语教学的作用和意义,探讨了如何就外语课堂否定反馈问题进行深层次调查研究。

Abstract

In the course of language learning, learners inevitably commit all kinds of errors for lack of linguistic knowledge and lack of proceduralized knowledge ready to be employed in performance. According to behaviorists, language learning is a process of habit formation. As symptoms of failure, errors are supposed to be eliminated from the classroom altogether. With the development of cognitive theories and deeper understanding of the learning process, errors begin to be viewed as tools facilitative to learning. Research findings have indicated that provision of positive feedback only will cause some erroneous forms to exist in interlanguage lastingly, thus resulting in fossilization. This suggests the importance of negative feedback. Actually negative feedback is not only necessary but also effective in that it can help learners make cognitive comparisons, adjust their hypotheses and hasten the speed of second language incorporation.

To millions of Chinese university students, instruction is the major means to improve language proficiency. Therefore, teachers' corrective behavior has considerable impact on their interlanguage development. However, with most of research focusing on negative feedback in NS-NNS interactions and immersion classrooms, we have little knowledge of how negative feedback is provided in foreign language learning context. This book represents an attempt to discover teachers' corrective behavior in classrooms, individual students' needs and individual students' feedback provision in group discussions.

This book consists of five chapters.

Chapter One introduces briefly the research background and purpose of writing.

Chapter Two is about definition of errors, attitudes towards errors, evaluation of errors, judgment of error gravity, types of errors and causes of errors. Judgment of errors can be based on three criteria: correctness, appropriateness and acceptability. The causes of errors of competence include interference of L1, intralingual transfer, misconception – including teaching and use of communicative strategies. On the other hand, the occurrence of errors of performance results from cognitive and psychological restrictions.

Chapter Three addresses such questions as definition of negative feedback, the necessity and effect of giving negative feedback and factors taken into account in error treatment, followed by a literature review of empirical studies investigating error treatment. Purpose of the activity, grammaticality of the learners' expressions, clarity of meaning, frequency of the occurrence of errors, language level of the students, their personality and affective needs are factors that count much when a teacher considers whether to give negative feedback or not.

Chapter Four states the purpose of the study and methodology employed, reports findings and discusses how often, what, how, when and who to treat errors in teacher-student interactions and student-student interactions. The subjects included eighty teachers from twelve universities and three hundred and fifty-two freshmen from five higher learning institutes. Data were collected by the administration of questionnaires and interviews. Findings were as follows:

1. Teachers did not over-react to students' errors. The type of errors they treated most frequently was expression errors. Next were grammatical errors and pronunciation errors. The techniques employed most by teachers were recast and elicitation. Some teachers made use of non-verbal means in providing negative feedback. Most of the teachers corrected student errors after the students finished with their expressions. Teachers' corrective behavior differed when students were engaged in teacher-centered activities and pair/group work.

2. The difference between EM teacher group and NEM teacher group mainly consisted in: 1) EM teachers corrected their students less often than NEM teachers. 2) EM teachers treated expression errors more than NEM teachers, while NEM teachers treated grammatical and pronunciation errors more. 3) EM teachers used clarification request more than NEM teachers, while NEM teachers used explicit correction and metalinguistic feedback more.

3. A majority of teachers did take individual differences into account in providing corrective feedback. They corrected LP students, female students, students with low self-esteem, low risk-takers and students with high level of language anxiety less often. They employed different means of correction to extroverts and introverts, HP students and LP students, students with high self-esteem and students with low self-esteem, high risk-takers and low risk-takers and students with high level of language anxiety and students with low level of language anxiety.

4. The students held a positive attitude towards errors and error correction. However, they did not want error to be corrected too frequently. Two types of errors put at the top of their priority list, which were worth great attention in error treatment, were pronunciation errors and expression errors. The students preferred corrective techniques leading to self-repair. English majors had a stronger desire to be offered the opportunities to correct errors by themselves. Students wanted their teachers to correct their errors upon their completion of expression. They approved of their teachers' different way of treating errors in whole-class activities and pair/group work. On the whole, teachers' corrective behavior could meet the students' needs.

5. The preferred corrective techniques of HP students, students with high self-esteem, high risk-takers and students with high L2 confidence were those leading to self-repair. For LP students, low risk-takers, students with high language anxiety level and students with low L2 confidence, their favorite corrective technique was recast.

6. Students' attitude toward peer correction was positive. They did not treat peers' errors frequently. They corrected their peers' pronunciation errors most often and recast erroneous expressions most often in peer correction.

7. HP students, extroverts, students with high self-esteem, high risk-takers, students with low language anxiety level and students with high L2 confidence tended to provide their peers with more opportunities for self-repair. LP students and students with low self-esteem often used recast. Low risk-takers and students with low L2 confidence liked to correct peers' errors explicitly.

8. In pair/group work HP students, extroverts and high risk-takers preferred corrective techniques leading to self-repair more than LP students, introverts and low risk-takers. Students with high language anxiety level were fond of recast, while students with low language anxiety level liked explicit correction best. Students with low L2 confidence preferred explicit correction, while students with high L2 confidence were in favor of recast.

Chapter Five is the conclusion part. Major findings are summarized. Included in this chapter are also pedagogical implications and limitations of the study.

Table of Contents

Chapter Four　Negative feedback in EFL classrooms

Chapter Five　Conclusion

Chapter One   Introduction

The beginning of the twenty-first century sees the great advancement of global economy. The close cooperation between countries in trade and culture entails the use of a second language as an effective means of communication. As is known to all, to get a good command of a foreign language requires not only one's determination and strong will to overcome various kinds of difficulties in the course of learning, but also optimal facilitative learning environment and conditions. When someone lives in a country where the second language is spoken, wide exposure to the target language and abundant opportunities to contact native-speakers will enable him to gain linguistic knowledge and improve language skills in everyday life without much difficulty. However, for an overwhelming majority of people, especially Chinese, they are not so lucky to get access to the ideal learning environment. Instruction, therefore, turns out to be crucial for their language learning. Such factors as teaching materials, means of instruction, importance attached to the accuracy and fluency of language use and theoretical basis of instruction all lead to different outcome of learning.

In the course of moving forward through developmental stages, language learners inevitably commit various kinds of linguistic errors in an attempt to use the target language. Since instructors are facilitators of the learning process, their belief in language learning and teaching will have profound influence on their attitude toward learners' errors and thus affect their "corrective reactions" (Chaudron 1986). It has been widely accepted that errors play a significant role in the language learning

1

process, as Corder pointed out more than three decades ago. They are indicators suggesting to what extent the language learners have grasped the target language system and in what aspects they are in need of help (Corder 1967). Upon the occurrence of linguistic errors, the appropriate way of treating them will greatly facilitate learning. Up to now, however, no deep-probing investigation as to how errors are treated in the foreign language context has been carried out. Hopefully, my research will provide the instructors in China with a clear picture of how negative feedback is given in EFL classrooms and what are the students' needs and wants. With this in mind, we can take effective measures to improve teaching quality. For the sake of limited time and space, I will confine my report to treatment of linguistic errors made in classroom interactions, including conversations between teacher and students and discussions among students in doing pair work or group work.

This book consists of five chapters. Chapter One is the introduction part. Chapter Two is about definition of errors, attitudes towards errors, evaluation of errors, judgment of error gravity, types of errors and causes of errors. Chapter Three addresses such questions as definition of negative feedback, the necessity and effect of giving negative feedback and factors taken into account in, followed by a literature review of empirical studies providing negative feedback. Chapter Four states the purpose of the study and methodology employed, reports findings and discusses how often, what, how, when and who to treat errors in teacher-student interactions and student-student interactions. Instructive suggestions are made on these questions. Chapter Five is the conclusion part. Major findings are summarized. Included in this chapter are also pedagogical implications and limitations of the study.

Chapter Two　Errors

2.1　Definition of errors

Linguists and researchers differ in their definition of linguistic errors. Dulay, Burt and Krashen (1982) defined errors as the deviation from a selected norm of language performance. As for Chun, Day, Chenweth and Luppescu (1982) and Richards, Platt, J. and Platt, H (1992), errors referred to the use of a linguistic item in a way that, according to fluent users of the language, suggested faulty or incomplete learning. The definition given by Liski and Puntanen is somewhat ambiguous: "an error occurs where the speaker fails to follow the pattern or manner of speech of educated people in English speaking countries today" (Liski and Puntanen 1983:227). In Lennon (1991)'s study, he employed a more cautious definition: an error is a linguistic form or combinations of forms which, in the same context and under similar conditions of production, would, in all likelihood, not be produced by native speaker counterparts. As suggested by these definitions, errors are forms deviated from a norm. The norm is generally considered to be native speakers' proper use of the target language.

2.2　Attitude towards errors

People's attitude toward linguistic errors varies from negative to affirmative. According to behaviorists, language learning is a process of habit formation, the association of particular stimuli with particular

3

responses. It is believed that second language acquisition is similar to L1 acquisition and two effective means of helping learners to form the stimulus-response associations consist in imitation and reinforcement. The aim is that good habits can be developed through drills until they become automatic. Therefore, in behaviorists' opinion, the occurrence of errors is undesirable, for they reflect incomplete learning. As symptoms of failure, errors are supposed to be eliminated from the classroom altogether.

By contrast, mentalists hold a different view. They do not regard learners as passive receivers of knowledge, who can improve language skills only through imitation and mechanic practice. Mentalists recognize the active role the learners play in the learning process. In their opinions, learners are attempting to make sense of the linguistic evidence they are exposed to and trying to get solutions to those problems they encounter in the learning process by applying what they know about their native language, the second language and other languages they have learned before as well as their general knowledge about the world. Errors occur when the learners make faulty hypotheses about the use of target language items and rules. In this case errors are considered to be the evidence to suggest that learners are working their way out for the correct use of the target language. Therefore, errors are not harmful, but helpful to the learning process. With the advancement of cognitive theories and further investigation of second language learning process, this viewpoint has gained wide acceptance by linguists and language teachers (Ghadessv 1985; Murphy 1986; Norrish 1983; Pasty & Nina 1993; Richard & Rod 1990).

2.3 Evaluation of errors

When evaluating language learners' utterances, people will consider whether the expressions are in conformity with the target language rules.

Correctness or *well-formedness* is the most frequently used criterion used to judge the presence of errors. However, as Corder (1981) pointed out, the superficial well-formedness of an utterance does not necessarily mean that an error was absent. According to him, the utterances of a learner can be classified into three categories: *superficially deviant*, *superficially well-formed and appropriate in the context and superficially well-formed but inappropriate*. Similar to first two types of utterances, the third type is deviant from the target language usage rules. There are also errors in these utterances because of their inappropriateness. In addition to *correctness* and *appropriateness*, *acceptability* is another criterion for error evaluation. Those expressions that are correct but unlikely to be used by native speakers cannot be regarded as expressions free of errors (Lennon, 1991).

2.4 Types of errors

When the word "error" is mentioned, another word "mistake" will pop into our mind. Under many circumstances in our everyday life these two words are used interchangeably as synonyms. However, in the field of second language acquisition, when one word is deliberately chosen, the implication is clear: the meaning is unique and cannot be replaced by another. When the learners use incorrect, inappropriate or unacceptable items for lack of knowledge, *errors* have been made. They indicate the learners' lack of "competence" (Chomsky, 1965). By contrast, when the learners know the rules but unable to produce correct words or sentences because of fatigue, inattention, anxiety or slips of tongue, these devious items are termed *mistakes* (Corder, 1967). They reflect learners' unsatisfactory "performance".

In terms of linguistic categories, errors can be divided into phonological errors, syntax and morphology errors, lexical errors and discourse errors. *Phonological errors* refer to those concerned with mispronunciation or inaccurate intonation. Some language learners are unable to pronounce vowels and consonants properly. Some may have difficulty in word stress, sentence stress, rhythm or intonation. *Syntax and morphology errors* are grammatical errors concerned with sentence structure, tense marker, agreement, gender and voice marker. *Lexical errors* result from improper use of words in the context. Confusion of words similar in form or meaning is the major factor accounting for the occurrence of lexical errors. It was reported that a considerable proportion of learners' errors are of this type (Grauberg, 1971; Meara, 1984). The utterances with lexical errors may be grammatically correct, but ambiguous in meaning or unacceptable to native speakers. Another type of error, *discourse error*, refers to those errors that involve violation of rules in language style and organization.

On the basis of surface strategy taxonomy, there are errors of omission, addition, misformation and misordering. When an item that is an indispensable part of a well-formed utterance is absent in an utterance, the error is *omission error*. Language learners tend to omit grammatical morphemes more frequently than content words, especially the copula, past tense and third person markers. *Addition errors* are characterized by the presence of an item that ought not to appear in a well-formed utterance. It was reported that three types of addition errors have occurred in the speech of language learners: double marking errors, regularization errors and simple addition errors (Dulay et al., 1982). *Double marking errors* appear when two items are marked for the same feature. *Regularization errors* arise when learners apply the rules for producing regular forms to irregular ones. Other additional errors that do not belong to these two types are termed *simple addition error*. In addition to omission error and addition error, another type of errors, *misformation error*, is caused by inappropriate use of language form or structure. As mentioned by Dulay et al. (1982), three types of misformation errors have been frequently reported: regularization errors, archi-forms and alternating forms. *Regularization errors* are those in which regular markers are used in place of irregular markers. *Archiforms* refer to the improper use of one of a class of forms to represent others in the class. With the development of language proficiency, learners also tend to use various members of a class alternatively. Such errors are termed as *alternating forms*. Another type of error that frequently occur in learners' language is *misordering error*, which is characterized by misplacement of a morpheme or several morphemes in an utterance. Such errors can often be found in embedded questions produced by language learners.

With regard to communicative effect, errors can be categorized into two types: global errors and local errors. *Global errors* such as missing sentence connectors and wrong order of the major constituents affect overall sentence organization. They may impede meaning conveyance and hinder comprehension. In contrast, errors in verb inflections, auxiliaries and articles only affect single constituent of a sentence. They are termed *local errors*. Such errors do not often lead to communication breakdowns.

Errors can also be divided into pre-systematic errors, systematic errors and post-systematic errors according to the stages in which errors are made. Three stages have been identified by Corder (1977). In the pre-systematic stage, the learners only have a vague idea that the target language is a system. They produce items from random guesses. When errors are committed, they have no awareness and cannot correct them. In the systematic stage, learners come to know rules of the target language, but they cannot apply the rules in a proper way. Upon the occurrence of errors they still cannot correct by themselves. With the growth of linguistic knowledge, the learners step into the third stage, post-systematic stage. In this stage errors are relatively infrequent. When their attention is drawn to errors, the learners can not only correct them but also explain why they should be corrected in that way.

7

A deviant expression is either overtly erroneous or covertly erroneous. When the constituents or the overall sentence structure of an utterance do not conform to the target language rules, *overt errors* occur. By contrast, if a superficially well-formed utterance appears to be inappropriate in the particular context, the error is termed *covert error*. The classification of overt errors and covert errors is based on correctness of the surface level of utterances.

What's more, errors can be divided into several types according to their causes. Dulay et al. (1982), mentioned four types of errors: *developmental errors*, those similar to errors made by children learning the target language as the first language; *interlingual errors*, those resulting from the influence of L1; *ambiguous errors*, those belonging to either category; *other errors*, those belonging to neither. Upon the review of several studies, Richards (1998) made a distinction between interlingual errors and intralingual errors. *Interlingual errors* mainly result from language transfer. In contrast, the origin of *intralingual errors* consists in the target language itself. They reflect how learners manage to assimilate new knowledge into their existent language system and apply what they have acquired to practical use when requested to do so. According to Richards, subcategories of intralingual errors include overgeneralization, simplification, developmental errors, communication-based errors, induced errors, errors of avoidance and errors of over-production. James (1998) classified errors into four categories: interlingual errors, intralingual errors, communication strategy-based errors and induced errors. The classification has obtained wide acceptance. Detailed description will be given in Section 2.6.

2.5 Judgment of error gravity

Khalil (1985) mentioned in his article three widely used criteria in error gravity evaluation: intelligibility, acceptability and irritation.

Intelligibility refers to the extent to which the expression with errors can be comprehended. *Acceptability* concerns the seriousness of the error. *Irritation* reflects the emotional reactions of an addressee. A wealth of research has investigated native speakers' judgment of learners' language errors. It was found that NS judges tend to regard lexical errors as more serious than grammatical errors, that global errors interfere with comprehension more than local errors, that the substitution of marked for unmarked forms are considered to be more severe than errors in which unmarked forms replace marked forms and that sentences with omission or wrong choice errors are more difficult to understand than sentences with insertion errors (Burt, 1995; Tomiyama, 1980; Khalil, 1985; Santos, 1987). Compared with native speakers, non-native speakers tended to be more severe on the whole (Hughes and Lascaratou, 1982; Davies 1983; Sheorey, 1986). They were very hard on errors in tense, agreement, prepositions and question formation, but their judgment of lexical and global errors was more lenient (Davies, 1983; Sheorey, 1986). NNS judges appeared to be influenced by their belief in language learning and factors relating to a particular context, while NS judges based their evaluation largely on how an error influenced their comprehension.

2.6   Causes of errors

2.6.1   Errors of competence

As mentioned before, errors of competence are those resulting from lacking of required L2 knowledge. To realize the presence of these errors and correct them is beyond the students' current ability. When these errors are pointed out, the learners have no idea why they are unacceptable. The causes of errors of competence include interference of L1, intralingual transfer, misconception-inducing teaching and use of communicative strategies.

2.6.1.1 Interference of L1

When exposed to quantities of target language materials or requested to communicate with the target language, learners tend to apply what they know about their native language to the unfamiliar foreign language contexts. As Jackson (1987) pointed out, interference occurred as an item or structure in the second language manifested some degree of difference from, and some degree of similarity with the equivalent item in the learner's first language. Influence of L1 can be found at all levels: phonology, syntax, lexis, pragmatics and morphology. Proponents of contrastive analysis contended that items that were similar in the L1 and L2 would be easier to learn than those that were different. However, later research indicated that interlingual similarity might also create difficulty (Laufer, 1992; Granger, 1996; Keys, 2002). According to Eckman's (1977) markedness differential hypothesis, a target language form would be difficult to learn if its L1 equivalent was different and if the target language form was marked or more marked. Findings of research suggested that errors arising from L1 interference occurred more frequently in phonological and lexical levels of language than in the grammatical level and that influence of L1 on certain areas of grammatical level acquisition tended to be more remarkable (Grauberg, 1971). Interlingual errors were found to be more common in adult learners than child learners (Dulay and Burt, 1974; White, 1977). They were considered to decline with proficiency. Meaning-oriented learners are thought to be less prone to transfer their L1 knowledge in performance than form-focused learners (Benson, 2002).

2.6.1.2 Intralingual transfer

Linguistic studies revealed that a large proportion of errors could not be traced to negative transfer of L1 (Richards, 1971; Haded, 1998). As Gass (1984) and Selinker (1992) contended, another source of errors is target language itself. Learners may intentionally make use of existent knowledge in the target language when requested to fulfill receptive and productive tasks. They may transfer what they have learned in the target language to new learning situations. When the learners have no idea of rule restrictions and extend rules to inappropriate contexts, overgeneralization errors arise. Such overgeneralization errors as *heros*, *destroied*, and *watchs* are epidemic among Chinese learners. There are also times when learners reduce the redundant part of a sentence, which lead to the occurrence of simplification errors. A point in case is statement forms used as questions. Since the presence of simplification errors may not be impediments for people to achieve their purpose of communication, they are not so noticeable to both error producers and their audience. Therefore, this type of error has the liability to last for a long time and fossilize. Besides overgeneralization and simplification, other factors such as misanalysis, hypercorrection and false concepts are also likely to result in intralingual errors.

2.6.1.3 Misconception-inducing teaching

Stenson (1983) first used the term *induced errors* to refer to those errors that resulted more from classroom instruction than from L1 interference or from incompetence in the target language. Sometimes textbook writers fail to exemplify a language rule in a clear and comprehensive way. When learners are exposed to the new linguistic materials, they are likely to make incorrect induction or incomplete generalization. For example, the overemphasis on use of one tense or one type of clause may put students in the danger of overusing them and therefore slow down their progress in walking through developmental stages. Besides, as imparters of linguistic knowledge, language teachers often introduce new language items and structures to the students. Implicit or imprecise explanations on the usage may cause the learners to make false analogy and commit errors. Take, synonyms, for example. The words "sick" and "ill" are often introduced as synonyms. When the students encounter the sentence "He can't come to class today

11

because he is ill", their teacher may tell them that the word "ill" can be replaced by "sick", for they have the same meaning. Later in students' production we may find such an error as *an ill man*. Because the teacher has not told the students "ill" cannot replace "sick" when modifying a noun, the students form the misconception that they can be used interchangeably in all contexts. Thus problems arise. What's more, to ensure that learners get high scores in English examinations, teachers may simplify some language phenomena to provide the students with "applicable rules". Errors inevitably occur when the learners apply these rules to exceptions. Another problem worthy of note in foreign language contexts is concerned with teachers' production of the target language. Since foreign language learners do not have so much exposure to the target language as second language learners do, teachers' talk serves as an important source of language input in the students' learning process. Though teachers are supposed to have a good command of the target language, they, as non-native speakers, may make errors occasionally for lack of knowledge, fatigue or poor physical condition. When the students do not realize the presence of errors in their teachers' speech, they may take it for granted that what the teachers say is acceptable standard target language. After absorbing faulty knowledge into their interlanguage system, learners may commit errors in their production.

2.6.1.4 Use of communication strategies

To make up for incompetence, the learners tend to use communication strategies to achieve effective communication. As Yue (1999) defines, a communication strategy is the conscious employment of a verbal or nonverbal mechanism for communication when precise linguistic items are not readily available to the learner. The learners may coin words, use synonyms and opposites, switch to L1 or literally translate L1 items into L2 when they are in need of expressing certain ideas. When some items are inappropriately used, communication

12

strategy-based errors arise. It was revealed that compared to natural acquirers, learners receiving formal instruction were more likely to recourse to L1 in the presence of communicative problems (James and Persidon, 1993). The reason may be that these learners' interlocutors, their teachers and fellow students, share the same first language background with them and so they may successfully put themselves across by employing strategies concerned with the use of L1.

2.6.2 Errors of performance

Errors of performance, or *mistakes*, cannot be regarded as the indicators of learner's incomplete linguistic knowledge. Though the linguistic forms used by learners are deviant or inappropriate on the surface, it does not mean that correct forms or proper usage was out of the students' reach. Learners are capable of correcting errors by themselves as long as they are aware of the existence of mistakes. The occurrence of this type of error often results from cognitive and psychological restrictions.

2.6.2.1 Cognitive restrictions

According to information processing theory proposed by McLaughlin et al. (1983), the learning process requires the integration of many subskills. To meet the challenge of tasks, it is of great importance for automatic processing to occur. To reduce analytic burden, some underlying skills should be performed without conscious attention. When involved in communicative tasks, the learners need to think about what to express, organize these ideas, put them into words and order them in a way conforming to the target language rules. All these things should be done almost at the same time. Since the subdivisions of conversational skill are still under the domain of conscious processing, they will each occupy some of the learners' attentional resources. With primary attention on conveyance of meaning, the learners' attention on processing the employed linguistic forms is very limited. Their control of grammar

13

and language accuracy is therefore affected, which leads to the occurrence of mistakes. In the course of giving the speech, some learners may be able to perceive their mistakes. Some may not. This is mainly determined by the learners' processing ability and language proficiency. Nevertheless, whether they are aware of the mistakes or not, the learners have the ability to correct them if requested to do so. Apart from the reason mentioned above, memory lapses and lack of relevant attention to language forms resulting from fatigue and distractions may also account for the occurrence of mistakes.

2.6.2.2 Psychological restrictions

When holding conversations with others in public, a person is likely to have the feeling of *communication apprehension*, a type of shyness characterized by fear of or anxiety about communicating with people (Philips, 1992). Research on second language acquisition suggests that this type of apprehension is prevalent in language classrooms and is more severe when the learners speak a second language (McCroskey, 1977; Foss and Reitzel, 1988; MacIntyre and Garder, 1991). According to Tobias (1979, 1986), anxiety might affect learning in three aspects: input, processing and output. When performing a task, anxious learners may be engaged in cognition about their reaction to the task rather than concentrating on the task itself. The limited cognitive resources relevant to the task will produce deficits in learner's performance. Intrusion upon the long-term memory retrieval may lead to occurrence of mistakes.

Chapter Three　Provision of
negative feedback

3.1　Negative feedback

When the language learners produce incorrect, inappropriate or unacceptable expressions, their interlocutors, sometimes the native speakers in natural communicative circumstances, sometimes language teachers and fellow students, may react in various ways. They may ignore the existence of errors and continue with communication. They may rephrase the speakers' words to make meaning clear. Or they may employ verbal and non-verbal means to indicate difficulty in comprehension and request clarification. According to Vigil and Oller (1976), learners get two kinds of information from their interlocutors: cognitive information as to the use of the linguistic code and affective information as to whether the learners' contributions are valuable and worthwhile. These two kinds of information are termed *cognitive feedback* and *affective feedback* respectively. Vigil and Oller suggested that positive affective feedback is crucial for learners to make further attempts in communication. With positive affective feedback as the prerequisite, negative cognitive feedback is needed to provide the learners with the information that their utterances require reformulation.

When conducting studies in negative feedback, researchers have employed different terms to refer to negative cognitive feedback upon the occurrence of linguistic errors. Schachter (1984) used the term *negative input* to refer to the information provided to the non-native speakers that there was something wrong in what they just said. It was found that such negative input varied from simple expression of noncomprehension to explicit correction. The term *corrective feedback* is employed by Day et al. (1984), to refer to the appropriate items supplied by native speakers in response to what they perceived to be errors committed by non-native speakers. According to Crookes and Rulon (1988), *feedback* was the correct use by a NS of a grammatical instruction to suggest that some items had been used incorrectly in an immediately preceding NNS utterance. As for Lin and Hedgcock (1993), feedback describes the linguistic and metalinguistic information provided by target language speakers to learners about the grammatical accuracy of their spoken interlanguage. *Negative feedback* suggests to the learners that their hypotheses about the target language are incorrect, incomplete or unacceptable. Negative feedback may be classified into two types: explicit or implicit. They can also be termed as *overt* and *covert error correction* respectively (Oliver, 1995). It was found that both types of feedback were provided to second language learners (Nystrom, 1983; Mito, 1993).

3.2　Necessity and effect of negative feedback

According to cognitive theory, learning is a process of problem solving. It takes place when the learners employ means of analogy, induction and generalization to absorb new information to existent cognitive structure of knowledge. They form hypotheses about the system of the target language. Since the linguistic input learners obtain is limited and the formation of hypotheses is based on their existent incomplete knowledge, it is inevitable that some faulty hypotheses are constructed. Negative feedback suggests to the learners that there ought to be alteration of their hypotheses and guides them to reconstruct their

16

linguistic knowledge system. In cognitive theorists' view, learning requires negative feedback to help the learner to readjust their interlanguage system to move closer to the target language system.

Some researchers strongly argued for the provision of negative feedback. Allwright (1975) suggested three decades ago that learner errors should be corrected if learners could not correct by themselves. Higgs and Clifford (1982) and Hammerly (1987) pointed out that language learners exposed to natural acquisition environment and communicative language teaching without error correction and focus of form would hardly progress when they reached a certain developmental stage. According to the researchers, these learners might speak fluent language, but their speech might be full of linguistic errors. Compared with learners receiving form-focused instruction, some types of errors tend to exist much longer in these learners' expressions. White (1990) contended that positive evidence alone was not sufficient for learning to occur. Negative evidence should be provided to the learners, especially when some rules in the learners' native language shared some properties with the target language but were more general than the target language rules. Allwright and Bailay (1991) mentioned *notice the gap* principle, which refers to the notion that it is of great importance for learners to notice the difference between their production and the native speakers' speech in order to move ahead in the interlanguage continuum. Long (1996) emphasized the important role played by negative feedback from another perspective. As he stated, for redundant, communicatively and perceptually nonsalient items and infrequently occurring forms, there was little chance for learners to incorporate them into their language system if learners fail to pay adequate attention. In this case negative feedback can arouse learners' awareness and lead to learning.

Research evidence has accumulated to show that negative feedback can enhance language development. In an overview of the research conducted at that time, Hendrickson (1978) concluded that correction

17

of errors that impede communication, stigmatize the learner or occur frequently did improve the proficiency of EFL/ESL learners. Later empirical studies also proved that negative feedback succeeded in helping learners to make cognitive comparison (Nelson, 1987), modify their hypotheses (White, 1991) and promoting learning (Carroll and Swain, 1993; Nobuyoshi and Ellis, 1993; Richardson, 1993; Oliver, 1995; Doughty and Varela, 1998; Muranoi, 2000; Ayoun, 2001; Han, 2002; Philp, 2003; Ishida, 2004). In reviewing several studies, Ellis (N. Ellis, 1995) drew the conclusion that provision of negative evidence did improve the syntactic ability of classroom language learners. Research findings also revealed that second language learners provided with corrective feedback outperformed those learners in the control group, who did not receive negative feedback (Lightbown and Spada, 1990; Carroll, et al. , 1992; Mackey and Philp, 1998). Mito (1993) compared the effect of models and recast on locatives and adjective order learning for foreign language learners of Japanese. There was no learning of either structure in the modeling condition, but statistically significant improvement was found on both structures in the recast condition. Long, Inagaki and Ortega's (1998) study on L2 Japanese and Spanish learners lend further support to the notion that implicit negative feedback can be more effective than models, preemptive positive input, in achieving at least short-term improvements in structure learning. The studies conducted by Herron and Tomasello (1988) and Tomasello and Herron (1989) also revealed that negative feedback was more facilitative than positive evidence.

3.3 Factors taken into consideration in providing negative feedback

Upon the occurrence of an error, the teacher has several options: to treat or to ignore; to treat immediately or to delay; to transfer treatment

18

or not; to transfer to another individual, a subgroup or the whole class; to return or not to original error maker after treatment; to permit other learners to initiate treatment; to test for the efficacy of the treatment. The decision as to whether to give negative feedback is always an instantaneous one. In a moment the teacher may have to take several factors into account. Purpose of the activity, grammaticality of the learners' expressions, clarity of meaning, frequency of the occurrence of errors, language level of the students, their personality and affective needs are all factors that count much.

3.3.1 Purpose of the activity

In our English class language teachers still pay considerable attention to the development of learners' knowledge on sentence structures. After a certain rule of the target language has been illustrated, the students may be required to use the structure in the following interactive activity. At that time great weight will be attached to the accurate use of the language feature. It is necessary for the teacher to provide immediate negative feedback to a student when an error occurs suggesting incomplete knowledge of the target language structure, for the activity serves to reinforce what has been taught. Neglect of such errors may result in the stabilization of incorrect forms in learner's language system and possibly leads to fossilization. By contrast, in free conversations without linguistic foci, errors on some items or structures may not attract close attention.

3.3.2 Degree of deviation

Errors vary in degree of deviation, degree of violating norms of grammaticality and appropriacy. Some erroneous expressions may have incomplete sentence structure, random word combination and missing main verbs. These global errors inconsistent with the basic rules of a target language system may affect the overall structure of sentences. If

19

the errors are not corrected, the learners' further development may be obstructed. What's more, when learners use expressions unacceptable with regard to social conventions or offensive to the native speaker interlocutors, it is necessary for the teacher to point the errors out. If the use of target language has detrimental effect on relationships between people, modifications should also be made in the learners' production and their knowledge system.

3.3.3 Clarity of meaning

As is known to all, language is a means of communication. The erroneous use of some items or rules may not result in misunderstanding or confusion. Certain errors, for example, the improper use of articles, missing $-s$ to suggest plural form and misuse of singular verb form for plural nouns, may not baffle listeners' comprehension in some situations. Whether to correct them or not does not make much difference. However, the presence of other errors may impede communication and lead to failure of meaning conveyance. Take the sentence *He liked academic calendar* for example. This is an expression used by a non-English major student when the teacher asked him why the author of a text wanted to be a teacher. People will undoubtedly get confused on hearing such an expression. What the speaker really means to say is that the author likes to have free time in summer and winter vacation every year. Since we are all Chinese, we can translate the sentence into Chinese, the learner's native language, and make out the meaning. However, for English native speakers and people from other countries, they may find it puzzling. Therefore, for those errors obscuring meaning conveyance, immediate negative feedback in class is obviously of vital importance.

3.3.4 Frequency of occurrence

Some types of errors, especially grammatical and lexical errors, may frequently occur in language learners' utterances. For example, we often hear such an expression *They are lack of money to....* When the students express their opinions on some social phenomena or explain reasons for something to happen, the ill-formed phrase *be lack of* is used with high frequency. It is not produced by one student, but by several students. When errors like this appear recurrently in several students' performance, they are worth the teacher's attention. To enable the learners to have a better understanding, the teacher can illustrate the use of some language items or structures with examples after providing negative feedback. If necessary, opportunities for further practice can also be provided to the learners for the purpose of reinforcement.

3.3.5 Learners' language proficiency

Language learning is a process of knowledge accumulation and skill improvement. As the learners move forward in the interlanguage continuum, their linguistic knowledge increases and their cognitive processing ability improves. This enables them to avoid making some errors and get a higher degree of sensitivity of linguistic errors. Some grammatical and lexical errors are indicators of scanty knowledge for the poor students, but denotes lack of automatization for the good learners. Therefore, on considering whether to treat students' errors, the teacher should take learners' proficiency into account. When an error arises in a poor learner's speech, it may be necessary for the teacher to provide negative feedback to prevent fossilization. However, for a good student who has already passed through the developmental stage and has the ability to correct an error by himself/herself, the teacher may just choose to ignore the mistake and continue with the lesson. On the other hand, some errors committed by high proficiency students may require correction, while the same errors made by low proficiency students are supposed to be ignored. According to Pienemann's teachability hypothesis (Pienemann, 1985, 1989, 1999), it is of no use providing students with instruction when the linguistic knowledge is out of their

21

reach.

Besides, the techniques employed by the teachers in treating learners' errors should be different with regard to the students' proficiency. For a good student with high awareness of errors, the teacher may use recasts or clarification requests for correction, or simply provide the students with negative cognitive feedback by making nonverbal responses, such as shake of the head, frowning or expression of surprise or confusion. By contrast, when the error producer is a poor student, the teacher should be cautious to choose corrective techniques. Explicit correction may be more effective for them, which should be accompanied by a smile or praise in order not to discourage the student. If necessary, detailed explanation should be given in or after class to prevent errors from arising again.

3.3.6 Affective factors

Malinowski (1923) noted that all human beings have a need for phatic communion, a need to define oneself and find acceptance in expressing self in relation to valued others. People obtain senses of self-esteem from their experiences with others and from assessments of the outside world around them. According to Coopersmith (1967), self-esteem refers to the evaluation the individual makes and customarily maintains with regard to himself; it expresses an attitude of approval or disapproval, and indicates the extent to which an individual believes himself to be capable, significant, successful and worthy. Self-esteem is a personal judgment of worthiness expressed in the attitudes one holds towards oneself. As is known to all, no task can be successfully fulfilled without self-esteem, belief in one's own capabilities for that activity. As a type of negative feedback, error correction may become a threat to a person's self-esteem and affect his/her self-evaluation. In a position valued by the students, the teacher's critical attitude in error correction may intensify the grave situation. Friendliness and patience is of essential importance to ease the tension and irritation caused by negative feedback. If the teacher can give the student positive affective feedback and praise their contributions when treating the student's errors, the student may be more likely to benefit from the teachers' corrective behavior.

3.3.7   Personality of learners

Besides the difference in language proficiency, learners also differ strikingly in personality. As mentioned above, people need to have a feeling of acceptance to achieve success when they are involved in cognitive activities. Compared with fellow students with high esteem, learners who have relatively low esteem tend to be more sensitive to others' reflection to their performance. Negative evaluation from the teacher or peers may have a detrimental effect on them to result in despair and recession from further participation in learning tasks. For these learners, it is advisable to give them encouragement constantly and not to correct them too frequently. Another factor worthy of note is the student's anxiety level. Some students are extremely anxious when asked to answer questions in class. This may have something to do with their traits, their evaluation of their own ability and the specific contexts. For highly anxious students, they are so preoccupied with the thoughts of their feelings that they can spare little attention to other things. Therefore the nonverbal feedback provided by the teacher may be completely ignored. Even the verbal feedback may escape their attention. On treating these students' errors, the teacher may employ explicit corrective techniques when the students finish with their expression and calm down. What's more, correction of errors committed by extroverted students can be more direct and more frequent than those made by introverted students. The extroverts are relatively less easy to get frustrated after receiving negative feedback. Besides, students' risk-taking level may also lead to different needs and preferences.

3.3.8　Other factors

In addition to the factors mentioned above, there are other factors worth noticing in feedback provision. When errors are concerned with the use of high frequency words or expressions, they require treatment even though such errors do not lead to communication problems. Since these high frequency words or expressions are encountered constantly in everyday life, errors on them should be avoided as much as possible. Besides, because time for instruction is limited, correction should take up as little time as possible on condition that corrective behavior is effective. Moreover, classroom atmosphere is another factor to be considered. A sense of humor on the part of the teacher is highly valued by students. If errors are treated in an interesting and humorous way, it can not only benefit the students in their linguistic development but also provide them with the motivation to learn language well when they find the learning process so amusing and stimulating.

3.4　Empirical studies on provision of negative feedback

3.4.1　How often errors were treated

Much research on frequency of negative feedback provision has focused on the interactions between native speakers and their non-native interlocutors. Generally speaking, native speakers did not correct the linguistic errors in their non-native partners' talks frequently.

Gaskill (1980) involved his subjects in two types of conversations for his study: artificial and natural. The artificial conversation data was collected from four five-minute taped conversations between an Iranian nonnative speaker of English and four native speakers of American English. While the learner was talking to the native speakers on certain topics, a researcher was present to take notes and operate the recording equipment. Besides artificial conversations, the Iranian learner was also required to record ten-minute natural conversations between him and two native speakers he often contacted. Analysis of the approximately thirty minutes of taped conversation revealed that very few other corrections occurred. In fifty pages of transcript, only seventeen instances were related to other-correction. It was found that abundant morphological, phonological, lexical and syntactical errors went without being checked.

After analyzing 15.1 hours of recorded conversations between twenty non-native speakers and their native speaker friends in social settings, Chun et al. (1982). learned that only a small percentage (8.9%) of NNS errors were corrected by their native partners. What's more, they found it interesting that subjects of low proficiency received more corrections than those of high proficiency. As suggested by the results, 13.4% of the beginning students' errors and 3.0% of the advanced students' errors were treated. In their further study, the researchers chose 11 advanced ESL learners and 9 beginning/intermediate learners as subjects. Each learner was required to record two conversations with their NS friends outside the classroom at different times. On analyzing 12.7 hours of taped NS-NNS conversations, they found that of the 1575 NNS errors, only 117 (7.3%) errors were followed by NS corrective feedback. In every hour of classroom interaction there were on average 23.6 instances of on-record feedback to the beginning/intermediate subjects, while only 4.1 instances to the advanced students.

Crookes and Rulon (1988) selected audio-tapes of three communication tasks performed by 15 adult NS/NNS dyads. First, pairs spent about three minutes on free conversation to get to know each other. In the second task the names of four items were given to the participants. They were asked to reach an agreement as to the category that would include all but one of the items. In performing the third task, subjects were separated by a screen, with a pair of pictures similar but not identical in each side. The learners were required to describe the pictures to each other so as to identify the difference between the pictures. By using ANOVA to analyze the transcriptions of the audio-tapes, the researchers found that native speakers did not correct NNS speech errors frequently, but they provided significantly more feedback in the latter two problem solving conversations than in free conversation. The mean ratio of the second and third task was 0. 45 and 0. 32 respectively, while that of the free conversation is only 0. 07. Besides, the second task involved a significantly greater amount of modification of errors and incorporation of feedback than the first.

In Oliver's (1995) study, eight nonnative speakers selected from four primary schools in Perth, Western Australia were paired with eight native speakers to form dyads. It was revealed that errors or unclear NNS turns were more likely to get treated than they were ignored. A majority of errors (61%) received implicit negative feedback, while 39% were ignored.

When examining adult native-speaker/nonnative-speaker interactions in a nonclassroom setting, Braidi (2002) found that 25. 56% of the incorrect utterances were followed by negative feedback. Mackey et al. (2003). explored the effects of interlocutor type on the provision of feedback. It was found that 47% of nontargetlike expressions were responded to in adult NS-NNS interactions; 42% in child NS-NNS interactions. For NNS-NNS interactions, the adult dyads received feedback 32% of the time; the child dyads, 39% of the time.

In language classrooms several studies have also been conducted to investigate how frequently errors were corrected. It was suggested that a large proportion of learner errors were not treated (Courchene, 1980; Swain and Carroll, 1987; Long, 1988).

Nystrom (1983) examined teacher-student interaction in bilingual classrooms. After analyzing twenty-four hour of videotape data, she found that four teachers she studied differed in the way they provided negative feedback. Two of them corrected students' errors on 76% of the time. One teacher treated 87% of the errors. However, in the other teacher's class, no corrective feedback was provided to the students for the errors they made.

Since it was believed that language forms could be best learned when the learners' attention was focused on meaning, content-based approach to language teaching was set up. There was also research carried out in meaning-focused classrooms. Beretta (1989) reported an evaluation study of the Bangalore project. Analysis of 21 lesson transcripts indicated that 211 out of 327 linguistic errors (65%) were treated. Significantly more content errors received attention than linguistic errors. Lyster and Ranta (1997) examined teachers' corrective feedback in four French immersion classrooms at the primary level. They found that the students' errors treated by these four French teachers accounted for 69%, 49%, 67% and 62% of the total number respectively.

When investigating the relationship between interactional context and feedback, Oliver and Mackey's (2003) categorized teacher-learner exchanges into four types: exchanges focusing on content, communication, management and explicit language. It was found that more than eighty percent of non-target-like utterances in the explicit language context attracted feedback, which was significantly more than other contexts.

In foreign language learning context, Fanselow (1977) found in Spanish FL classroom that 22% of the learners' errors were left uncorrected. However, the findings of Doughty (1994) were different from that of Fanselow. In Doughty's report of her pilot study done in Australia, it was suggested that teachers provided feedback on 43% of the erroneous student turns.

Some insightful studies have also been conducted to examine the attitude and preferences of language learners concerned with error correction. Cathcart and Olsen (1976) administered a questionnaire to

27

ESL language learners receiving classroom instruction. These learners were found to like corrective feedback and want more of it. Seventy-five percent of the subjects wanted correction all of the time. However, these learners changed their minds when nearly all their errors received correction. They stated that constant correction deprived them of the opportunity to think coherently without interruption. The survey done by Chenoweth et al. (1983) also suggested that the NNSs generally developed a positive attitude toward error correction and they wanted significantly more correction from their NS friends than they reported receiving. When comparing the attitude of international ESL students and their teachers towards error correction, McCargar (1993) found that all student groups except the Japanese group considered it necessary for their teachers to correct every error they made. For another item "teachers should point out student errors without correcting them", only Koreans mildly agreed. All the other groups show clear disagreement. The responses of 1,431 Colombian and US foreign language learners in Schulz's (2001) study obtained similar results. Students were shown to have a strong belief on the positive role played by corrective feedback in FL learning. They also expressed marked preference for error correction in class.

3.4.2 What types of errors were treated

When reporting research findings of error treatment, researchers categorized language errors in different ways. Gaskill (1980) divided the errors made by an Iranian non-native speaker of English into four categories: morphological errors, phonological errors, lexical errors and syntactical errors. In investigating NS-NNS interaction Chun et al. (1982) classified NNS linguistic errors as word choice errors, syntactic errors and omissions. They did not include pronunciation errors in their study, since they found it "difficult to distinguish errors in pronunciation from systematic nonnative phonological patterns which prevail throughout the speech of NNSs (Chun, et al. 1982:539). Day et al. (1984) found that NS negative feedback was given to the non-native speakers after inappropriate pronunciation, lexical and syntactic errors, or errors of fact and discoursal usage. The means of categorization employed by Lyster and Ranta (1997) was somehow unique. They recognized phonological, lexical and grammatical errors. What's more, they made a separate category for errors in grammatical gender because of their frequency.

In Nystrom (1983) study, she asked the four teacher teaching bilingual classes to identify their students' errors and classified these errors into six types: phonological, lexical, morpho-syntactic, discourse, dialect and content errors. It was revealed that errors committed by students in four classes had different distribution patterns. Teacher A-1 identified a large number of errors of form, including phonological errors (28. 8%), lexical errors (35. 6%), morpho-syntactic errors (8.9%), discourse errors (11. 1%) and dialect errors (6.7%) and a small number of content errors (8. 9%). Students in Teacher A-2's class were found to commit syntactic errors (36.9%) and discourse errors (36. 9%) frequently. Besides, phonological errors accounted for 21. 7% of the total number. Only a few lexical errors (2%) and content errors (2%) occurred. As for Teacher B-1, 83% of the errors recognized by her were dialect errors. The rest were phonological and lexical errors. In Teacher B-2's class, the most frequently committed errors were phonological errors (37%). Other types of errors decreased in frequency as follows: dialect errors (21%), content errors (15%), lexical errors (13%), discourse errors (8%) and morpho-syntactic errors (6%). The problem with Nystrom's study is that some student errors might go unrecognized and the four teachers under investigation might have different norm of judgment. It is also a pity that the treatment of different types of errors was not studied.

The studies carried out by Chun et al. (1982) and Chenoweth et al.

(1983) helped to shed some light on the issue of how different types of errors were treated in NS-NNS interaction. In their studies errors made by non-native speakers were divided into five types: discourse errors (errors beyond sentence level), factual error (errors concerning factual knowledge or truth value of utterances), word choice errors (those involving incorrect choice or addition of a noun, verb, adjective, adverb, preposition, question word or other types of functional words), syntactic errors (errors of tense agreement, morphology and word order) and omissions (errors involving the incorrect omission of nouns, verbs, auxiliaries, articles or other words required by rules of standard English grammar). It was found that factual errors attracted most of native speakers' attention. They were corrected 89.5% of the time. What came next in the rank list were discourse errors. Thirty-five percent of discourse errors received treatment. Among the linguistic errors, 15% of the word choice errors were followed by negative feedback. Only 7% of syntactic errors received native speakers' attention. There was little correction of omissions (2.5%). Afterwards the researchers combined instances of word searches and NNS' requests for help with word choice correction. They obtained a higher percentage of word choice correction: 25.8%. A chi-square test suggested that word choice errors were corrected significantly more often than grammatical errors. In a later study (Chenoweth et al., 1983) questionnaires were distributed to students studying ESL in three English programs. Analysis of self-reported data indicated that these learners were corrected most often in the areas of pronunciation and word choice, less frequently in word form and word order errors and finally for factual accuracy.

Lyster (1998a) investigated the relationships between error types and feedback types in four French immersion elementary level classrooms. Nine hundred and twenty-one errors were coded as grammatical errors, lexical errors, phonological errors and unsolicited uses of L1. Corrective feedback moves are classified as negotiation of

30

form, recast and explicit correction. It was found that 80% of lexical errors, 70% of phonological errors, 56% of grammatical errors and 43% of uses of L1 received negative feedback. A great proportion of feedback moves following grammatical errors and phonological errors were recasts (64% and 72% respectively). The majority of lexical errors triggered negotiation of form. Use of L1 was followed by translation equivalents (50%) and negotiation (38%). Further analysis revealed that the interaction between error type and feedback type was significant. It turned out that teachers' negative feedback on lexical errors differed significantly from their choice of feedback on grammatical errors and phonological errors.

Another study investigated what areas of language the students considered important to receive correction from their teachers. The ESL learners surveyed by Cathcart and Olsen (1976) thought that pronunciation errors should be worth greatest attention of the teachers. Followed in the priority list were grammatical errors.

3.4.3 How errors were treated

Several researchers have examined the strategies employed by native speakers in correcting their non-native interlocutors' speech errors. Chun et al. (1982) recognized two strategies employed by NSs: on-record correction, which involved provision of correction with declaratory intonation, and off-record correction, which was ambiguous and was open to more than one interpretation as a correction or as a continuing contribution to the conversation. It was found that on-record corrections accounted for 125 of the 189 NS corrections (66%). A chi-square test revealed that on-record correction was used significantly more often than off-record correction. In their later study (Day, et al; 1984), the researchers got similar results. Instances of on-record corrective feedback (85) were found to be greater than off-record corrective feedback (32). Besides, a significant difference was found in the

31

amount of on-record feedback provided to two learner groups under investigation. The beginning/intermediate learners received significantly more on-record feedback than advanced subjects. Two types of NS-initiated NNS-completed repair were recognized in the study: clarification requests and confirmation checks.

In Oliver's (1995) study of interaction pattern in child NS-NNS, two forms of NS modification were identified when the native speakers provided reactive and implicit negative feedback to the NNS: negotiation strategies, including repetition, confirmation checks and clarification requests; recasts, which were defined as redisplay of the learners' utterance, with the syntactic structure reformulated maintaining the central meaning. The results suggested that the grammaticality and ambiguity of the nonnative learners' speech triggered different responses from native speakers. Negotiation appeared to be prompted by such errors as the incorrect use or omission of auxiliary, copula, pronoun, word choice, word omission and subject omission, whereas errors in plurality or subject-verb agreement were more often followed by recast. In response to an ambiguous NNS turn, negotiation occurred more frequently than recasts. What's more, most negotiation was found to follow NNS turns with multiple errors, while recast occurred more often in response to single-error utterances. Evidence also suggested that negative feedback had been noticed by non-native speakers, which resulted in the incorporation of correct linguistic forms into their language system.

Schmidt and Frota (1986) reported how Schmidt learned Portuguese as a second language in both tutored and untutored situations in Brazil. Schmidt claimed that hearing correct versions immediately following his erroneous expressions helped him notice the gap between his interlanguage and the target language and was, therefore, beneficial. He claimed that informal correction such as confirmation checks and clarification requests did not have strong impact on his learning.

Carroll and Swain (1993) have explored the effects of various types of negative feedback on the learning of generalizations. One hundred adult Spanish-speaking learners of English were divided into five groups, including four treatment groups and one comparison group, twenty for each. On making an error, subjects in Group A were given explicit metalinguistic information about the rule they were to learn, while those in Group B were just told that their responses were wrong. When committing errors, Group C subjects were provided with an implicit reformulated correct response. For Group D subjects, they received indirect metalinguistic feedback when there was a problem in their response. They were asked whether they were sure of their answer. The comparison group, Group E, received no treatment. The results suggested that all treatment groups performed better than the comparison group in initial feedback session, first recall session and second recall session. Besides, Group A, the group who was supplied the explicit rule, outperformed all the other four groups.

In their quasi-experimental study on the development of interrogative constructions, Spada and Lightbown (1993) provided ESL learners in two experimental classes with nine hours of form-focused instruction and negative feedback over a two-week period. Three teachers in two experimental groups and the comparison group were found to differ considerably in the types of corrective feedback they provided. One of the experimental teachers gave students matalinguistic feedback 81% of the time. The other experimental teacher tended to repeat learners' incorrect production (55%) or provide explicit error correction (34%). In contrast, the comparison teacher was the one who used implicit feedback most frequently (31%). She seldom provided students with metalinguistic feedback or repeated their incorrect production, but preferred to use other types of explicit correction (52%).

In language classrooms an early study was conducted by Chaudron

(1977) to examine how negative feedback was provided by three French immersion teachers teaching subject matter and French language arts classes in Grades 8 and 9. From the analysis of the transcripts, Chaudron found that teachers' reduced repetitions of students' errors were more likely to lead to students' correct responses than expansions or elaborations of the learners' responses or direct provision of the correct forms.

Nystrom (1983) investigated how teachers dealt with their students' errors in bilingual classrooms. Teacher A-1 responded to her students' errors by modeling the desired student statement, repeating the error, prompting the student, telling the student exactly what to say, or transferring the corrective role to other students. In her repetition of the errors, sometimes she would change their forms and sometimes emphasized with stress or pitch the changes that had been made. Teacher A-2 and Teacher B-2 followed the same basic pattern as Teacher A-1: soliciting, modeling, prompting, and drilling. Teacher B-1's response was different from the other three in that she did not treat any errors she identified in the videotapes. In the study Nystrom recognized three feedback styles in these teachers' treatment of student errors: overt corrective, covert corrective and noncorrective.

The focus of Lyster and Ranta's study was to find out what techniques were employed by four French immersion teachers and how frequent these techniques were employed (Lyster and Ranta, 1997). On analyzing transcripts of classroom interaction taken from 14 subject-matter lessons and 13 French language arts lessons, they found that among the six feedback types (explicit correction, recast, elicitation, metalinguistic feedback, clarification requests and repetition), recast was the most popular technique used by the teachers, which comprised 55% of the engative feedback. The other five types of feedback distributed in decreasing frequency as elicitation (14%), clarification request (11%), metalinguistic feedback (8%), explicit correction

(7%) and repetition (5%). Besides, analysis of students' uptake, which was defined as "students' utterance that immediately followed the teacher's feedback " (Lyster and Ranta, 1997:49), suggested that all instances involving elicitation led to students' uptake. Clarification request, metalinguistic feedback and repetition were also effective in eliciting uptake from students (88% , 86% and 78% respectively). By contrast, only half of the explicit correction moves and 31% of the recast moves resulted in learner uptake. Further study suggested that negotiation of form was more effective in eliciting immediate repair, especially for grammatical and lexical errors (Lyster, 1998a). It was also revealed that recasts were very likely to be confused with noncorrective repetition in meaning-oriented classrooms, because they fulfilled identical functions. What deteriorated the situation was that recasts and noncorrective repetitions were frequently accompanied by positive feedback to indicate the approval of the content of the message.

Recast seemed to be the most frequently employed negative feedback employed by teachers. Beretta's (1989) study on Bangalore project also suggested that the most common strategy for treating linguistic errors was repetition with change (36%). Oliver and Mackey (2003) found that 47% of ESL learners' non-target-like expression's were followed by recast in explicit language-focused exchanges. In Basturkmen, Loeuer and Ellis's (2004) case study investigating the relationship between teachers' stated beliefs and their classroom practice of focus on form, it was revealed that two teachers employed recast 57.7% and 58% of the time respectively. This technique was used more often than other error correction types.

Besides the investigation on error treatment in classroom teacher-student interaction, some researchers set out to examine how learners provide each other with negative feedback in pair work and the effect of such response. Morris and Tarone (2003) reported their study on ten beginning foreign language learners of Spanish who registered for the same Spanish class at a university. The target structure was the Spanish third-person singular form of present tense indicative verbs. Participants were required to complete a jigsaw task in pairs. They also took pre-, post- and delayed posttests. To elicit the learners' perception of the feedback they received upon the occurrence of errors, Morris administered a stimulated recall session for each participant. Three categories were coded as corrective feedback: explicit correction, recasts and negotiation, which might take the form of clarification requests, metalinguistic clues, elicitation and repetition. It was revealed that interpersonal conflict and negative social interaction taking place in pair work had deleterious effect on some learners' perception of implicit negative feedback provided by their peers. Learners' expectations on being negatively evaluated socially by their more proficient partners might prevent them from incorporating the implicit negative feedback into their interlanguage system.

An early study conducted by Cathcart and Olsen (1976) investigated ESL students' opinions on negative feedback provided by their teachers. Findings suggested that learners preferred explicit correction of their oral errors. To detect students' preferences for feedback on their speech errors, Kaufmann (1993) administered questionnaires to second language teachers and students in Puerto Reco and Turkey. Descriptions and examples of twelve types of feedback ranging from explicit to implicit were provided. It was revealed that for grammatical errors and pronunciation errors, teachers tended to give implicit feedback, while students preferred to receive explicit feedback. Afterwards students were required to fill in another questionnaire to state their opinions on what responses from their non-teacher interlocutors were considered appropriate upon the occurrence of speech errors. The students regarded it acceptable for their friends to overlook their erroneous expressions, but they required corrections from their teachers.

Besides verbal feedback provided to learners upon the occurrence of non-target-like utterances, a non-verbal feedback technique was proposed by Schachter (1981), which comprised a set of hand signals indicating tense/aspect/voice error, agreement error, errors in pluralization, preposition errors, word order errors and errors in articles. She suggested that non-verbal hand signals could be employed as an alternative when verbally transmitted information was ineffective.

3.4.4 When errors were treated

Corrections can be provided on the spot, which usually involved interruption of the speakers conversation. They can also be given after the speaker finishes with a whole sentence or the whole expression. In language classrooms sometimes treatment can be delayed to later occasions when it is appropriate to analyze or explain in detail how to correct similar errors or errors of the same type. Up to now only one study, that of Day et al. (1984), has addressed this question. They found that in native-nonnative discourse native speakers tended to show politeness in providing corrective feedback. Sixty-seven of seventy-two instances of NS corrective feedback on errors made by the beginning/ intermediate students were given at transition points. It was suggested that NS corrective feedback occurred significantly more often at a transition point than as an interruption.

3.4.5 Who corrected errors

When language errors occur in learners' speech, their interlocutors may choose to provide negative feedback by themselves or transfer the responsibility of correction back to the learners or to other audiences. Up to now two studies have been done to investigate who corrected the errors: one by Day et al. (1984) in natural interactions and the other by Lyster & Ranta (1997) in French immersion classrooms. Day et al. (1984) found in their study that there were times when NS-initiated NNS-completed repair occurred. Clarification request and confirmation checks were used by NSs in response to the NNS errors or to clear up conversational misunderstandings.

In Lyster and Ranta's (1997) report of French immersion classroom study, teachers were found to use explicit correction and recast to provide the corrective feedback 62% of the time. They also employed such means as elicitation, clarification request, metalinguitstic feedback and repetition to provide students with the opportunities to correct errors by themselves or by their peers. Analysis of *uptake*, the students' utterance immediately following teachers' feedback, suggested that these four strategies succeeded in triggering student-generated repairs. Findings revealed that elicitation led to 43% of all student-generated repairs. Metalinguistic feedback, clarification requests, and repetition were respectively responsible for 26%, 20% and 11% of the remaining self-generated repairs.

Chapter Four   Negative feedback
in EFL classrooms

4.1   Purpose of the research

The review of existent empirical studies suggested that a great proportion of research on error treatment centered on native speakers' negative feedback to the errors occurring in non-native speakers' utterances. Several studies have been carried out in language classrooms, but the subjects were mostly bilingual and immersion program participants. Among the scanty research conducted in foreign language context, such questions as how different types of errors are treated, the corrective techniques employed by teachers, to what extent students are allowed to take the responsibility for the correction of their own errors and when errors were treated have not been dealt with. No research has been carried out to help us obtain a clear picture of how often, how, when and what types of student errors are treated by their teachers and peers when learners are engaged in pair work or group work. Furthermore, with regard to students with different proficiency level, personality, risk-taking level, language anxiety level and L2 confidence, no one has investigated the distinction among these students in their attitude toward and preferences of error correction. Whether the teachers have met the individual students' need is also a question to be explored. Though it is impossible to get a comprehensive picture of negative feedback provision in EFL classrooms from one study, my research represents a primary attempt to address this question. The purpose of my study is to find out how linguistic errors occurring in classroom interactions are treated in teacher-centered and learner-centered classroom activities in intensive reading class, how students, English majors and non-English majors who differ in proficiency level and personality, think of error correction, how they treat each other's errors and whether the way teachers treat student errors fit the students' needs.

My research questions are as follows:

1. How do intensive reading teachers correct their students' errors (how often, what, how, when, and who) in teacher-centered classroom activities and pair/group work? Is there any difference between English majors' teachers and non-English majors' teachers in providing negative feedback? Do teachers take individual differences into account when providing students with corrective feedback? How?

2. What are the students' attitudes towards their errors and error correction in teacher-centered and student-centered classroom activities? How do students treat their peer's errors when they are involved in student-centered activities? Is there any difference between English majors and non-English majors in their attitudes and behavior? Is there any difference among students with different proficiency, personality, risk-taking level, language anxiety level and L2 confidence?

3. As far as error treatment is concerned, to what extent can teachers' behavior match the students' needs and wants?

4.2 Methodology

4.2.1 Subjects

The subjects of this study include 80 English teachers. Forty teachers teaching English majors comprehensive English course (EM

40

teachers) were from nine universities. The age of EM teachers ranged from twenty-six to fifty-seven, with an average of 32. 1. There were 11 mail teachers and 29 female teachers. Forty teachers teaching non-English majors intensive reading course (NEM teachers) were from twelve universities. These teachers aged from twenty-five to fifty-eight, averaging 30. 5. Fifteen of them were male, twenty-five, female. Five EM teachers and five NEM teachers were interviewed later, including 4 male teachers and 6 female teachers.

Three hundred and fifty-two first-year students participated in the present study. Half of them were English majors from four universities. Another half, non-English majors were from four universities. Twenty-seven male students and one hundred and forty-nine female students constitute the English-major group. One hundred and seven male students and sixty-nine female students make up the non-English major group. After the analysis of questionnaires, twenty English majors and twenty non-English majors were interviewed. Among them there were representatives of high-proficiency students, low-proficiency students, extroverts, introverts, students with high self-esteem, students with low self-esteem, high risk-takers, low risk-takers, students with high language anxiety level, students with low language anxiety level, students with high L2 confidence and students with low L2 confidence.

4.2.2 Instruments

4.2.2.1 Questionnaires

Based on the pilot study carried out on English teachers and students of the same educational background and proficiency level in a university, I made some necessary changes to the questionnaires designed for teachers and students. The questionnaire for teachers consisted of two parts: blank filling and open-ended questions. There were eighteen blank filling questions and three open questions. The questionnaire for students consisted of three parts: five-point scale test,

41

blank filling part and open-ended questions. For the first part, students were required to fill in the brackets following 26 statements with figures ranging from 1 to 5, with "1" representing "This is not true to me at all" and "5", "This is true to me absolutely". This part was to measure students' self-esteem, risk-taking, language anxiety, L2 confidence, awareness of errors and their attitude towards error correction. The second part included thirty-three questions. The first fifteen items in this part were quoted from Wen (1996) to find out whether a person was extroverted or introverted. The rest eighteen questions were about students' attitudes towards errors, their preferences of error correction and how they treated their peers' errors. The students were asked to give their answers by filling in the blanks with the choices they made. In the third part there were three open-ended questions. The students were required to express their opinions on whether all errors should be treated by the teacher, how they liked to have their errors treated and whether non-verbal means of correction should be employed by the teacher. To ensure that wording of the statements and questions would not lead to confusion or misunderstanding, questionnaires were written in Chinese, the subjects' native language.

4.2.2.2　Interviews

In the interviews with the teachers, I asked them specific questions concerned with language teaching and their corrective behavior in the classroom. For students, I elicited their opinions on and preferences of teacher correction and peer correction. To ensure that all the interviewees could express their ideas clearly and accurately, I used Chinese in the interviews. All the interviews were tape-recorded and later transcribed for analysis.

4.2.3　Data collection

The questionnaires for teachers were handed to the EM and NEM teachers or sent to them by email. They were returned upon completion.

Ten EM teachers teaching comprehensive English course and eight NEM teachers teaching intensive reading course helped to distribute the questionnaires for students and collect them after the students finished with their answers. There were three hundred and seventy-six questionnaires available. For the convenience of statistical analysis, one hundred and seventy-six questionnaires from English majors and one hundred and seventy-six from non-English majors were taken into consideration. Twenty-four papers of non-English majors, chosen at random, were left out.

After finishing with the analysis of the questionnaires, I designed interview questions and interviewed ten teachers and forty students.

4.2.4 Data analysis

4.2.4.1 Teachers' and students' response to the questionnaires

With regard to teacher's responses to each question in the blank filling part, the frequency of occurrence of each choice was calculated. Detailed information provided by these teachers to explain for the reasons to make certain choices and their answers to open questions were analyzed and generalized.

As to the five-scale test of the questionnaire for students, I first used SPSS (Statistic Package of Social Science) to recode the students' answers to some items, checked the reliability scale (all $\alpha > 0.7$) and calculated the mean scores for students' self-esteem, risk-taking level, language anxiety level, L2 confidence, awareness of errors and attitudes towards error correction. In order to find out the influence of such factors as language proficiency, personality, language anxiety and L2 confidence on students' attitudes and behavior concerned with negative feedback provision, I sorted out two groups of students for comparison, Group H and Group L. Students with high self-esteem, high risk-taking level, high language anxiety level or high L2 confidence belong to Group H. Those of low esteem, low risk-taking level, low language anxiety

43

level or low L2 confidence were members of Group L. For each way of measurement, the scores of Group H were among the top 15%, while those of Group L were among the 15% from the bottom. Because some students had the same scores, the demarcation line was not on 15% exactly, maybe a little above or a bit below. The scores of those students in Group H were 4.25 or above for self-esteem (84 students altogether, including 47 English majors and 37 non-English majors), 3.43 or above for risk-taking (48 students altogether, including 26 English majors and 22 non-English majors), 3.4 or above for language anxiety (73 students altogether, including 27 English majors and 46 non-English majors), 4.0 or above for L2 confidence (68 students altogether, including 32 English majors and 36 non-English majors). The scores of students in Group L were 3.0 or below for self-esteem (48 students altogether, including 21 English majors and 27 non-English majors), 2.0 or below for risk-taking (62 students altogether, including 20 English majors and 42 non-English majors), 1.8 or below for language anxiety (53 students altogether, including 24 English majors and 29 non-English majors) and 2.4 or below for L2 confidence (58 students altogether, including 19 English majors and 39 non-English majors).

According to students' responses to the first fifteen items in blank filling part of the questionnaire, each choice in conformity to the characteristic of extroverts was given one point. Then the total score for each student was calculated. Following what Wen (1996) suggested, those students whose total score was above 12 were distributed to extrovert group, while those who scored below seven were considered to belong to introvert group. There were 42 students in extrovert group, including 19 English majors and 23 non-English majors. Introvert group numbered 80. Forty-three students were English majors; thirty-seven, non-English majors. For the rest of the questions in the second part of the questionnaire, I counted the number of the students who gave the same answer (s) to each question and calculated the percentage by dividing the number with the total number of students. As to open-ended questions, detailed information provided by the students were taken down and summarized. With regard to all the questions concerned with error treatment, comparison between English majors and non-English majors, Group H and Group L, extrovert group and introvert group was made.

In addition, I also grouped those students whose final exam scores ranked top fifteen percent of the EM group and NEM group together as high proficiency (HP) students. The scores of HP English majors were above 86; those of HP non-English majors, 83. There were 54 HP students altogether, including 25 English majors and 29 non-English majors. Another group, low proficiency (LP) student group, was composed of 74 students, whose final exam scores ranked fifteen percent from the bottom in EM and NEM group. The scores of LP English majors were lower than 74; those of LP non-English majors, 64. Forty-three English majors and thirty-one non-English majors constituted LP group. HP students' responses to questions on error correction were compared with those of LP students.

4.2.4.2 Transcription of the interview

The questions I asked in the interviews were not in the same order. Therefore, after making the transcriptions, I put the interviewees' answers to the same question together when analyzing the data to make it easier for comparison.

4.3   Results and discussion

4.3.1 How often errors were treated

4.3.1.1 Teachers' opinion and corrective behavior

As for the uncompleted statement in the questionnaire (See Appendix I) " You _____ correct your students' errors in class ",

45

there were five choices: ① always ② often ③ sometimes ④ rarely ⑤ never. EM teachers' responses were distributed like this: 10% chose "often", 82.5% chose "sometimes" and 7.5% chose "rarely". For NEM teachers, 7.5% of them made the second choice, 80% made the third and 12.5% made the fourth choice. It seemed that an overwhelming majority of EM teachers and NEM teachers did not treat student errors very frequently in their language class. There was not marked difference between EM teacher group and NEM teacher group on the frequency of error treatment.

To get more detailed information, I examined how teachers dealt with errors that were deemed necessary to receive negative feedback. There was one item in the questionnaire eliciting how often teachers treated students' errors in three situations: ① errors were treated in class ② errors were noted down and treated after class by talking with individual students ③ errors were taken down and systematic explanation and opportunities for practice were provided later. Teachers' responses to the questionnaire suggested that 20% of EM teachers and 27.5% of NEM teachers always or often provided negative feedback in class immediately. A majority of teachers (55%, including 47.5% of EM teachers and 62.5% of NEM teachers) sometimes did so. Twenty percent of teachers (32.5% of EM teachers and 10% of NEM teachers) stated that they rarely corrected errors immediately in class. Compared with NEM teacher group, EM teacher group seemed to correct their students less often in class. According to those teachers who chose to treat students' errors in class, they provided immediate negative feedback to students when the presence of errors impeded communication, when errors were prevalent in students' speech, when errors were considered serious or when errors were already noticed by other students and lack of treatment would be likely to mislead students to form faulty hypotheses. What's more, some teachers mentioned that they corrected errors in class immediately when there was sufficient time and the corrective behavior would not have deleterious effect on classroom atmosphere or hurt individual students' feelings.

Eight EM teachers (20%) and seven NEM teachers (17. 5%) often took the measure of treating errors after class by talking with students individually. This means was also employed by 21 EM teachers (52. 5%) and 25 NEM teachers (62. 5%) now and then. As some teachers responded in the questionnaire, they usually talked with some students after class over their errors when these errors did not lead to misunderstanding, when such errors occurred several times in the students' speech but could seldom be found in other students' utterances, when the errors could be detected and corrected by most students or when the error committer was an introvert lacking confidence.

Besides, 38. 8% of the teachers (37. 5% of EM teachers and 40% of NEM teachers) declared that they always or often noted down errors, explained why the usage was unacceptable and/or gave the students opportunities to practice later. Thirty-four teachers (16 EM teachers and 18 NEM teachers, 42. 5% of all the teachers) sometimes treated errors in this way. Such corrective behavior was usually triggered by the prevalence or recurrence of errors in students' speech.

To find out whether teachers' corrective behavior varied with regard to individual differences among students, I designed an item in the questionnaire: When the error producers belong to the following groups, will you treat their errors differently? extroverted vs. introverted students; male students vs. female students; HP students vs. LP students; students with high self-esteem vs. students with low self-esteem; high risk-takers vs. low risk-takers; students with high language anxiety vs. students with low language anxiety. Analysis of teachers' responses showed that the difference consisted in the frequency of error treatment in class and the way errors were treated. As far as frequency of immediate error treatment in class was concerned, it was found that introverts, female students, LP students, students with low self-esteem, low risk-takers and students with high language anxiety level received relatively fewer corrections from their teachers than extroverts, male students, HP students, students with high self-esteem, high risk-takers and students with low language anxiety. A large number of teachers mentioned that the request they set for LP students and students with low self-esteem was lower than other students. These students, together with introverts, female students, low risk-takers and students with high language anxiety were more likely to feel embarrassed and frustrated when they were corrected in front of the whole class. Therefore, some minor errors produced by these students were often deliberately ignored. Besides, many teachers reported that they preferred to talk with introverts, LP students, students with low self-esteem and students with high anxiety level over their errors individually after class.

Such factors as teachers' belief in language learning and teaching, their attitude toward errors and error correction and their observation of students' wants and needs tend to affect their decision on whether to treat learners' language errors in class. Elaborate investigation showed that EM teachers' opinions and corrective behavior were similar to those of NEM teachers in some aspects, but different in many other aspects.

1) Focus in instruction

EM teacher group and NEM teacher group seemed to have different focus in their instruction, which could be detected from their belief in language learning and teaching. EM teachers seemed to attach great importance to communicative function of language. In the course of teaching they created a large number of opportunities for students to put their linguistic knowledge to practical use. Though some questions for students to answer were concerned with comprehension of the texts, much time in class was devoted to motivating students to express their opinions on solutions to some problems in life. It could be perceived that language functioned as an effective means of transmitting information and conveying ideas. One male EM teacher made a strong statement:

"Language is a tool for communication. What we need is not only to help our students improve their ability to use language, but also to improve their ability to think, to think about life, to think about some problems in the society. If a student can only use very simple English to express very simple ideas, why should they further their study in English then?" When introducing new words and expressions, EM teachers place much emphasis on word usage in contexts. They introduced to students the use of different language styles under specific circumstances. In addition, they often called their students' attention to the cultural differences between English-speaking countries and China.

Two EM teachers told me that they would assign oral or written tasks to students after learning new words and expressions to help them know how to apply them to practical communicative situations. Students were asked to work in pairs or groups to make up dialogues or write articles with the new vocabulary included. Sometimes the students were also requested to use certain sentence structures, which might be the potential problems for students, say, subjunctive mood used for past events, in their conversations or compositions. Such activities made learning process more motivating. Students' interest was kindled when they found what they learned could be applied to real life. Furthermore, these tasks increased the students' awareness of the importance of using language appropriately.

Compared with NEM teachers, EM teachers seemed to be more severe with students in those language areas "which were not in accordance with the requirement for an English major", as one EM teacher pointed out. According to him, the commission of some pronunciation errors, grammatical errors and lexical errors would indicate that the learners failed to have a solid foundation of English. These learners' ignorance of the basic rules of language use, as was indicated by the occurrence of these errors, was considered to be unacceptable, since English majors were supposed to begin their future

49

career by displaying their remarkable language ability. They were expected to use English fluently, accurately and appropriately.

In contrast to EM teachers, NEM teachers did not pay much attention to the practical use of English as a foreign language. The reasons might consist in the belief of non-English majors' purpose in learning English and students' language ability. "Many of my students are reluctant to speak English. When some students are asked to answer questions, they just give very short answers. They do not have much confidence in using English. And perhaps they don't feel it necessary to do so," one NEM teacher said. When I asked NEM teachers whether they often raised questions concerned with social problems and people's life, their answers were negative. "I tried with some, but the result was far from satisfactory. Our students don't have sufficient vocabulary at their disposal. Some average students can only say a few words. Maybe they lack practice. You'll feel uncomfortable when you see the students stand there struggling for suitable words, very nervous. I mainly ask students questions related to the content of the texts," another teacher stated. NEM teachers devoted much time to analysis of text structure, checking students' comprehension of texts and explanation of language points in order to meet the request of CET 4. Some of class time was spent on vocabulary expansion for the teaching of each unit. Examples of the use of some new words were provided. Synonyms and antonyms of some nouns and adjectives were introduced. False friends were also distinguished sometimes. But it seemed that NEM teachers did not put as much weight on the contextual usage of words as EM teachers did.

Since non-English majors did not take English as their specialization, it was unnecessary for them to have very high language proficiency. They were not expected to have a command of English as well as English majors did. Some mistakes considered unbearable to English majors might not be corrected when they occurred in non-English majors' speech. However, NEM teachers' focus might be on some errors

50

ignored by EM teachers according to the request of the syllabus and their students' needs.

2) Attitude toward errors

An item in the blank-filling part of the questionnaire was about teachers' attitude toward language errors. The question was like this: "As for language errors, I agree that _____. ① Errors are indicators of failure, which should be avoided as much as possible. ② Errors are an important part of learning process, which play a positive role. " All of the EM and NEM teachers agreed to the second statement. When asked why he thought so, an EM teacher said, "The occurrence of errors is an unavoidable phenomenon. It proves that the students are making attempts in the course of learning, though the attempts are incorrect. Errors are very meaningful and important to our students' learning. They are worth attention and analysis. " Another EM teacher made a stronger point: "It's abnormal if one doesn't make mistakes. ... One will pay attention to the language item that he/she has used erroneously when he/she is exposed to new English materials. ... Also (a person can improve his language ability—*added by the author*) through the teacher's correction. He will know the proper use after the teacher corrects him. That's helpful. " An NEM teacher held the same opinion. He explained, "If students don't commit errors, the teacher won't know their problems. You cannot point them out. One will make mistakes when learning a language. He won't make progress without committing errors. "

3) Attitude towards error correction

The first open-ended question in the questionnaire was about the teachers' attitude towards error correction. They were asked whether they thought it necessary and important to treat language errors and why. An overwhelming majority of teachers (92.5% of EM teachers and 97.5% of NEM teachers) gave positive answers. According to them, negative feedback could speed up the learning process and shorten the time needed for moving along the developmental stages. It was an effective means to ensure smooth flow of communication and improve students' language ability, especially the accuracy of their language. Several EM teachers mentioned that it was of great importance to heighten the students' awareness of using language accurately and appropriately. "The students pay too much attention to fluency of language use. They do not care much about accuracy. An error will be difficult to eliminate if it exists for a long time to become a habit," one EM teacher stated. As suggested by other teachers, treating one student's error could also benefit his/her peers. Error treatment would enable both the error producer and the students in class to make timely adjustment of their incorrect hypothesis. The possibility of recurrence of errors will diminish. When confirming the effectiveness and importance of error correction, teachers also expressed their concern in teaching. They pointed out that errors should not be treated too frequently. That would undermine students' confidence and kill their interest in learning and using English. What's more, some teachers mentioned that different means of correction should be taken under different circumstances with regard to different types of errors and individual differences of students.

4) Focus in classroom interactions: form or meaning

In response to the blank-filling question asking the teachers of their focus when the students were engaged in classroom interaction, all the teachers except one EM teacher and one NEM teacher stated that they paid more attention to meaning conveyance than language forms. According to an EM teacher, the language ability of the first-year English majors was limited. Though the ultimate goal of English majors was to speak native-like English and it was essential for English majors to use the language accurately, emphasis on both form and meaning for the time being was impractical. Another EM teacher suggested, "Language is used as a tool for communication. What is important is to be able to express one's ideas with the language. Their [the students' — *by the author*] English will be more accurate with the development of

52

language ability and through more practice. " Non-English majors' lower language ability put their teachers in a more cautious position. "It's not so easy for our students to use English to express their ideas. Too much stress on form will intimidate them. Some students will never open their mouth again, " an NEM teacher said. Another NEM teacher expressed the same concern: "It is important to inspire students' confidence in using language. Too critical with their language will discourage them and undermine their confidence. "

　　5) Teachers' evaluation of learners' awareness of errors

　　The second item in blank-filling part of the questionnaire was like this: "When using English to express their opinions in class, your students can _____ realize their errors. ① always; ② often; ③ sometimes; ④ rarely; ⑤ never. " Fifteen percent of EM teachers chose "often", 75% chose "sometimes" and 10% chose "rarely". By contrast, NEM teachers' choice of "often" accounted for 7. 5% , "sometimes", 67. 5% and "rarely", 25% . It appeared that most EM and NEM students could sometimes perceive their errors. English majors' sensitivity to errors seemed to be a bit higher than non-English majors according to their teachers' report. This might have something to do these students' higher proficiency level and more attention to accuracy of spoken language. According to some teachers, their students might pause in the middle of an utterance or an expression, shook head, or rephrase what they had said. From this they knew that their students had already detected their errors. There were times that students quickly and readily make self-repair when the teachers gave hints. That was perceived to be an indication that the students could detect their errors. Several teachers also made the same statement that they found high proficiency students having a higher awareness of their errors than poor students. When asked what errors were likely to be realized by the students, teachers said that those errors resulting from slips of tongue because of anxiety or fatigue were most likely to be noted, for example, the confused use of "he" and "she", "his" and "her", the errors violating rules of subject and verb agreement, mixed use of verb tense and some lexical errors resulting from confused use of words with similar pronunciation.

6) Factors to be taken into account when deciding on whether to treat errors

There was one question in the questionnaire. The first part went in this way: "On deciding whether to treat student errors, people usually take the following factors into account. You put _____ in your priority list (please make one or two choices). Please rank order these factors according to their significance. Write down "1" in the bracket following the statement you think is the most important, "2" for the factor considered next to it. Put 1 to 7 in the brackets in this way. ① Whether the error will irritate the native speakers; ② Whether the error is related to what has just been taught or the focus of the present lesson; ③ Whether the error occurs frequently in students' speech; ④ Whether the expression with error(s) is frequently used in everyday life and whether other students will form misconceptions when the error is ignored; ⑤ Whether the error hinders communication and lead to misunderstanding or failure of meaning conveyance; ⑥ Whether the student can realize his/her error and correct by him/herself; ⑦ Individual differences among students; ⑧ others (please illustrate)." It was revealed that the factor considered to be of greatest importance was whether the error had deleterious effect on communication (see Table 1). Sixty-five percent of EM teachers and seventy percent of NEM teachers ranked this factor first. Put next in the priority list was "whether the error occurs frequently in students' speech" (45% of EM teachers and 35% of NEM teachers). Another factor attracting much attention was whether the language items or structures were high frequency expressions in everyday life. Twenty-five percent of EM teachers and thirty percent of NEM teachers were concerned about this.

Table 1   Factors to be considered most important in
deciding whether to treat errors

	EM teachers	NEM teachers	Total
1) whether irritating native speakers	7 17.5%	7 17.5%	14 17.5%
2) whether related to what taught or the focus of lesson	4 10%	8 20%	12 15%
3) whether occurring frequently in students' speech	18 45%	14 35%	32 40%
4) whether used frequently in everyday life	10 25%	12 30%	22 27.5%
5) whether hindering communication	26 65%	28 70%	54 67.5%
6) whether students can detect errors and self-correct	3 7.5%	4 10%	7 8.8%
7) individual differences among students	2 5%	2 5%	4 5%

There seemed to be no dramatic discrepancy between EM teacher group and NEM teacher group in their responses to this part of the question. However, detailed analysis of the way teachers ranked order these factors suggested that EM teachers seemed to concern more about the frequency of error occurrence, while NEM teachers paid more attention to whether the error was about language points taught before or

55

related to the focus of present lesson. Besides, though both groups did not consider the factor "whether the error will irritate the native speakers" to be as important as some other factors, EM teachers seemed to put more weight on it than NEM teachers. Furthermore, compared with EM teacher group, NEM teachers seemed to place more emphasis on individual differences among students.

Table 2　Factors concerned with students' individual differences: number of teachers who put them at the top of the priority list

	EM teachers	NEM teachers	Total
student's personality	9 22.5%	6 15%	15 18.8%
student's language proficiency	9 22.5%	12 30%	21 26.3%
student's self-esteem	13 32.5%	12 30%	25 31.3%
student's L2 confidence	7 17.5%	8 20%	15 18.8%
student's language anxiety	2 5%	2 5%	4 5%

The second part of this question was about teachers' corrective behavior with regard to individual differences among students. Teachers were asked to rank order the five factors, student's personality, student's language proficiency, student's self-esteem, student's L2 confidence and student's language anxiety according to the importance they attached to them in deciding whether to treat errors. EM teachers seemed to think that students' self-esteem was of greatest significance. Teachers who ranked this factor first accounted for 32.5% of the EM teacher group (see Table 2). Next to it was students' language proficiency and students' personality (22.5% and 22.5% of the EM teachers). In contrast, NEM teachers attached equal importance to students' self-esteem and their language proficiency. Teachers putting these two factors at the top of the list both took up thirty percent of NEM teacher group. What they considered to be less important was students' L2 confidence, followed by students' personality and their anxiety level.

It can be seen clearly that EM teacher group differed with NEM teacher group in their concern. EM teachers paid more attention to students' personality in treating their errors, whereas NEM teachers concerned more about students' proficiency. The reason may consist in the difference between English majors and non-English majors in their language proficiency and speaking ability. English majors have already possessed the capability to use English to put their meaning across, though their oral English is still not satisfactory. EM teachers do not have to care too much about their students' proficiency and L2 confidence. But for non-English majors, they have greater problems in expressing themselves accurately and fluently because of lower language proficiency and lack of practice. As an NEM teacher stated in the interview, the purpose of their present instruction was to motivate the non-English majors to speak English as much as possible in class, since it was not such an easy thing for many students to use English. According to her, caution should be taken in providing students with negative feedback, especially to those poor students. Too many corrections would extinguish the students' interest in learning English and lessen their esteem. Besides, as another NEM teacher contended, corrections were unnecessary on some occasions, for they were out of the reach of some students. "For those students who are very poor in English, they can't understand why you make a correction. The correction doesn't have any effect. It's just a waste of time," said he.

7) Frequency of treating errors when students were engaged in student-centered activities

As to the item "In whole-class activities and pair/group work, is there any difference in your decision as to whether to treat errors and how to treat errors? ① Yes ② No. The difference of whether to treat errors lies in _____ . The difference of how to treat errors lies in _____ ", the majority of the teachers (52. 5% of EM teachers and 77. 5% of NEM teachers) gave the answer " Yes ". Among these teachers, some responded that they treated errors more frequently when students were engaged in pair/group work. In whole-class activities they mainly concentrated on the content of students' speech. It was impractical for them to correct students' errors with regard to the limited time in class. Therefore, some minor errors might be ignored. When students were doing pair/group work, they could give timely negative feedback to the students so as to help them improve their accuracy. Besides, when students were corrected in front of the whole class, they might feel nervous and frustrated. In pair/group work, the audience was of a small size and atmosphere was relaxed. Teachers' correction would not cause students to feel embarrassed.

Contrary to the majority's corrective behavior some teachers behaved in the contrary way. They provided negative feedback less often in pair/group work. In these teachers' opinion, the purpose of designing pair/group work was to help students improve their ability of communicating with others in the target language. Therefore, only those errors impeding communication should be corrected. Another reason for these teachers to have such corrective behavior was that they thought error correction in whole-class activities was more effective. Since there was a larger audience, the correction of some common errors would help all students heighten their awareness of the errors.

8) Attitude toward peer correction

In response to the question whether they thought peer correction was helpful to language learning, most teachers' answer was positive. Fourteen teachers (17. 5%) strongly agreed to the idea that peer correction was beneficial. Those who agreed to the statement accounted for 61. 3% of the teachers (65% of EM teachers and 57. 5% of NEM teachers).

4.3.1.2   Students' needs and preferences

As the main body of the learning process, students have their own opinions and preferences. Therefore, a large number of questions were designed to elicit their needs and wants concerned with error treatment in class. Discussion on these questions will be given below.

1) Attitude towards errors

An item in the blank filling part asked the students whether they viewed linguistic errors as indicators of failure or as a facilitative factor in language learning. The wording of the question was the same as its counterpart in the teachers' questionnaire. Substantial quantities of students (84. 1% of EM students and 90. 9% of NEM students) agreed that errors were an indispensable part of the learning process and they played a facilitative role. As one EM student stated in the interview, if a person did not make mistakes, he/she did not know what was still in need of improvement, which did no good to language learning. A small number of students (15. 9% of EM students and 9. 1% of NEM students) made another choice for this item. For these students, the occurrence of errors suggested lack of linguistic knowledge or the required language ability. One NEM student said that she felt embarrassed and discouraged when errors were made. For these students, what they cared most was to avoid making errors.

2) Attitude towards error correction

In the first part of the questionnaire, five-scale test, four items were concerned with students' attitude towards error correction: ① I think it necessary to have errors corrected; ② I think error correction is helpful to language learning; ③ I don't think it's necessary to correct errors; ④ I don't think error correction is of great use. After recoding and checking reliability scale, further analysis revealed that the mean score for EM students and NEM students was 4. 45 and 4. 36 respectively. It could be seen that a substantial proportion of students (85.8% of EM students and 83.5% of NEM students) developed a positive attitude toward error correction (see Table 3). There was little difference between EM student group and NEM student group.

Table 3　Students' attitude toward error correction

	1.00-2.99 (negative)	3.00-3.99 (neutral)	4.00-5.00 (positive)
EM students	3 1.7%	22 12.5%	151 85.8%
NEM students	4 2.3%	25 14.2%	147 83.5%

3) Focus in classroom interaction: form or meaning

To find out what was the students' focus when opportunities were provided to them to practice spoken English, I asked them to make a choice as to the question "When using English in class, I pay more attention to ① language form; ② meaning to be conveyed." An overwhelming majority of the students (89.2% of EM students and 81.8% of NEM students) responded that they put more emphasis on the conveyance of meaning when speaking in English. In the interview students said that the function of language was to communicate to others what was in one's mind. According to them, if people could not let others know their opinions or transfer information to others, the effort of using language would be in vain.

4) Awareness of errors

In five-scale test four items were designed to find out sensitivity of students upon the occurrence of errors: ① I seldom detect errors in my speech; ② I can always detect the errors I have made; ③ I cannot find errors in my speech on many occasions; ④ I realize I have made errors after the teacher or my classmates point them out. After making

60

necessary statistical analysis, it was revealed that the mean score for EM students and NEM students was 3.33 and 2.997 respectively. There was significant difference between these two groups in error awareness. EM students had a higher awareness of errors than NEM students (p = .000, t = 5.136). From Table 4 it could also be seen that a large proportion of NEM students (42%) could rarely realize that they have committed errors, but only 18.8% of the EM students were in the same condition. The difference between the two groups could be attributed to English majors' higher language proficiency and relatively large amount of language input they have obtained.

Table 4   Students' awareness of errors in speech

	1.00-2.99 (low)	3.00-3.99 (medium)	4.00-5.00 (high)
EM students	33 18.8%	110 62.5%	33 18.8%
NEM students	74 42%	90 51.1%	12 6.8%

5) Necessity for errors to be treated by teachers in class

The first open-ended question of the students' questionnaire went like this: "Do you think it necessary for the teachers to treat all the linguistic errors? On what occasions should errors be treated? Why?" It was found that a great proportion of students (83.5% EM students and 74.4% NEM students) did not think it necessary for teachers to treat all the errors they committed. One non-English major said, "It's inevitable for us to make many errors. If the teacher corrects every error we make, we can't speak (in English) then. I think the teacher should treat some serious errors." The students held the opinion that some grammatical and lexical errors might hamper addressees' comprehension, even arouse irritation, and so these errors should be treated immediately in class.

61

Many students mentioned that errors resulting from inappropriate use of words or expressions should be taken seriously, for misconceptions would be detrimental to learning. Some students also pointed out that frequently-made errors and errors violating the fundamental rules of the language system were in need of treatment. A large number of students, especially English majors, stated that it was of no necessity for teachers to spend a lot of time in treating some mistakes resulting from slips of tongue or carelessness. In their opinions, teachers should treat those errors they could not detect and could not correct by themselves. For the small proportion of students (16.5% of English majors and 25.6% of non-English majors) who contended that all errors should be treated, error correction was of great importance to them. "If errors are not treated, we will make the same errors again and again. They will be erroneous all the time," a non-English major said. "How can I correct my errors if I don't know where they are?" another non-English major wrote. These learners took such a position because they did not want erroneous expressions to stabilize in the language system to be hard to correct just like a bad habit.

In response to the more detailed question "when the teacher notice my errors and considers it necessary to correct them, I usually want my teacher to _____. ① treat them in class; ② note down the errors and treat them after class by talking with me individually; ③ write down the errors and give us systematic explanation and practice later. Students who made the first choice, to have errors treated by the teachers in class, accounted for 68.2% of the total number (72.2% of EM students and 64.2% of NEM students). Those who wanted the teachers to talk with them over their errors individually after class took up 15.3% of the subjects (17% of EM students and 13.6% of NEM students). The rest 16.5% of students thought the teachers should illustrate the language points they had not grasped and provided them with further opportunities to practice. More non-English majors (22.2%) seemed to

62

be in need of such treatment than English majors (10. 8%). As two NEM students said in the interview, they sometimes could not understand the teacher's corrections. " It will be more helpful if the teacher can give us some examples and explain how to use the items in detail. We can have a clear idea," said one of them.

With regard to different needs of individual students, I analyzed the responses given by HP students and LP students, extroverts and introverts and students in Group H and Group L respectively. When both English major group and non-English major group were taken into account, there seemed to be no distinct difference between LP student group and HP student group. A majority of LP students (72. 2%) and HP students (75. 7%) wanted errors to be treated in class. However, there is a noticeable difference between LP students and HP students among non-English majors. More HP students wanted the teachers to treat errors in class (65. 5% of LP students and 77. 4% of HP students), while more LP students preferred the teachers to talk with them individually over the errors they made after class (20. 7% of LP students and 9. 7% of HP students). Among LP students, English majors seemed to develop more positive attitudes toward error treatment in class (80% English majors; 65. 5% non-English majors), while non-English majors were more fond of delayed treatment and systematic explanation (4% of English majors; 13. 8% of non-English majors). Whether the students were extroverts or introverts seemed to have no remarkable influence on their opinions on error treatment. More than seventy percent of extroverts (71. 4%) and introverts (77. 5%) responded that they wanted their errors to be treated in class. Nineteen percent of extroverts and fifteen percent of introverts found it more appealing for teachers to discuss with them over their errors after class. A few students (9. 5% of extroverts and 7. 5% of introverts) thought systematic illustration to be helpful. Students' level of esteem, risk-taking, language anxiety and L2 confidence did not lead to different responses to this question either. Most students (68.8% of students with low self-esteem and 71.4% of students with high self-esteem; 72.6% of low risk-takers and 72.9% of high risk-takers; 73.6% of students with low level of anxiety and 72.6% of students with high level of anxiety; 72.4% of students with low L2 confidence and 76.5% of students with high L2 confidence) preferred to have their errors treated in class. Some students liked to have talks with their teachers over their errors after class (16.6% of students with low self-esteem and 17.9% of students with high self-esteem; 11.3% of low risk-takers and 16.7% of high risk-takers; 18.9% of students with low level of anxiety and 16.4% of students with high level of anxiety; 13.8% of students with low L2 confidence and 17.6% of students with high L2 confidence). The students in need of systematic explanation constituted a very small proportion. For non-English majors under survey, more low risk-takers (19%) demanded systematic explanation than high risk-takers (4.5%), while more high risk-takers (77.3%) considered it appropriate to have errors treated immediately in class than low risk-takers (64.3%). As to students with low L2 confidence, more non-English majors (17.9%) were in favor of private talks after class than English majors (5.3%). Besides, non-English majors with low L2 confidence (12.9%) seemed to prefer systematic explanation of linguistic items than those with high L2 confidence (2.7%).

6) Attitude towards peer correction

Besides teacher-centered activities, pair work and group work play a significant role in helping students enhance language proficiency. Several items in the questionnaire were designed to explore how students view peer correction and how they treated each other's errors. The last item in blank-filling part of the students' questionnaire was like this: "'Peer correction is helpful to our study.' As to this viewpoint, I

_____. ① strongly agree; ② agree; ③ have no idea whether it is acceptable; ④ disagree; ⑤ strongly disagree. " More than a quarter of the students (31. 2% of the English majors and 26. 1% of the non-English majors) stated that they strongly agree that peer correction was helpful to their English learning. A majority of students (56. 3% of the English majors and 56. 8% of the non-English majors) declared that they agreed to the opinion. When asked whether they could accept negative feedback from peers, 38. 9% of the students (39. 8% of the English majors and 38. 1% of the non-English majors) responded that they could always accept and 57. 4% of them (56. 2% of the English majors and 58. 5% of the non-English majors) generally could accept. They regarded peer correction as a good opportunity to overcome their weaknesses and make improvement. " It is I myself who made the mistakes. Why don't I accept when they are pointed out?" an English major wrote. " I know they correct me out of kindness, not to laugh at me," a non-English major responded. Though holding a positive attitude towards peer correction, a few students were cautious in following their classmates' advice in error correction: "Those correct (suggestions) I will accept. There are some incorrect or improper (corrections) ," a non-English major stated.

7) How often errors were treated by peers in pair/group work

To investigate how often students treated each other's errors in pair/group work, I designed an item in the questionnaire: When engaged in pair work or group work, I _____ corrected my peers' errors. ① always; ② often; ③ sometimes; ④ rarely; ⑤ never. Five students (2. 3% of English majors and 0. 6% of non-English majors) chose " always". Thirty-six students (12. 5% of English majors and 8% of non-English majors) chose " often". These students held the opinion that it was of great importance to correct linguistic errors since the purpose of pair/group work was to improve language ability and errors without treatment would be "rooted" in one's language system and hard to erase. "Errors should be corrected," a non-English major stated. The majority of the students (61. 4% of English majors and 46. 6% of non-English majors) declared that they sometimes correct their peers' errors. For these students, correcting their classmates' errors would not only do good to their peers, but also benefit themselves in language learning. "For those errors that violate basic rules, I will correct them. When I correct others' errors, I will have a deeper impression (of the use of linguistic items)," a non-English major wrote in the questionnaire. Another non-English major expressed similar opinion: "If my correction is right, I will be very happy. I will have a kind of sense of achievement. At the same time I have also helped my classmates (with his/her study)." The reason why these students did not treat peers' errors frequently was that they themselves were not sure whether the use of some linguistic items or expressions was acceptable or not. "Sometimes I can't detect whether there are errors (in my classmates' speech)," a non-English major wrote. "On many occasions I myself don't know what is the correct way to express the ideas," an English major responded. Also about thirty percent of students (20. 4% of English majors and 42% of non-English majors) rarely correct their peers' errors. The major reasons were that they paid more attention to the content of their peers' expression and that they were not confident of themselves in their language ability. Students' responses suggested that compared with English majors, non-English majors were more concerned about their ability to detect others' errors and correct them. On the whole, it could also be seen that there was remarkable difference between English majors and non-English majors in frequency of peer correction. English majors corrected their peers' errors more frequently than non-English majors.

Table 5　Frequency of peer correction:
extroverts and introverts

	Always	Often	Sometimes	Rarely	Never
Extroverts (N = 42)	2 4.8%	10 23.8%	22 52.4%	8 19%	/
Introverts (N = 80)	2 2.5%	3 3.8%	40 50%	32 40%	3 3.8%

Table 6　Frequency of peer correction:
students with low self-esteem and students with high self-esteem

	Always	Often	Sometimes	Rarely	Never
Students with low self-esteem (N = 48)	/	1 2.1%	24 50%	21 43.8%	2 4.1%
Students with high self-esteem (N = 84)	2 2.4%	11 13.1%	45 53.6%	22 26.2%	4 4.7%

Table 7　Frequency of peer correction:
low risk-takers and high risk-takers

	Always	Often	Sometimes	Rarely	Never
Low risk-takers (N = 62)	2 3.2%	4 6.5%	20 32.2%	32 51.6%	4 6.5%
High risk-takers (N = 48)	/	5 10.4%	29 60.4%	12 25%	2 4.2%

Table 8　Frequency of peer correction:
students with low anxiety level and students with high anxiety level

	Always	Often	Sometimes	Rarely	Never
Students with low anxiety level (N = 53)	1 1.9%	10 18.9%	25 47.2%	15 28.3%	2 3.7%

(Continued Table)

	Always	**Often**	**Sometimes**	**Rarely**	**Never**
Students with high anxiety level (N = 73)	/	3 4.1%	36 49.3%	32 43.8%	2 2.8%

Table 9   Frequency of peer correction:
students with low L2 confidence and students with high L2 confidence

	Always	**Often**	**Sometimes**	**Rarely**	**Never**
Students with low L2 confidence (N = 58)	/	2 3.4%	27 46.6%	27 46.6%	2 3.4%
Students with high L2 confidence (N = 68)	1 1.5%	10 14.7%	36 52.9%	16 23.5%	5 7.4%

When the individual differences among students were taken into consideration, only proficiency did not appear to be the factor having great influence on frequency of peer correction (see Table 5, 6, 7, 8, 9). More than half of the students (55.4% of HP students and 55.6% of LP students) sometimes corrected their peers' errors. About thirty percent of students (28.3% of HP students and 35.2% of LP students) were rarely involved in peer correction. Students who chose " often" include 23.8% of extroverts and 3.8% of introverts, 13.1% of students with high self-esteem and 2.1% of students with low self-esteem, 10.4% of high risk-takers and 6.5% of low risk-takers, 18.9% of students with low anxiety level and 4.1% of high anxiety level and 14.7% of students with high L2 confidence and 3.4% of students with low L2 confidence. Students who chose " rarely" include 19% of extroverts and 40% of introverts, 26.2% of students with high self-esteem and 43.8% of students with low self-esteem, 25% of high risk-takers and 51.6% of low risk-takers, 28.3% of students with low anxiety level and 43. 8% of high anxiety level, 23. 5% of students with high L2 confidence and 46. 6% of students with low L2 confidence. It could be clearly seen that extroverts, students with high self-esteem, high risk-takers, students with low anxiety level and students with high L2 confidence provided more correction to their peers than introverts, students with low self-esteem, low risk-takers, students with high anxiety level and students with low L2 confidence.

4.3.1.3 Discussion

Analysis of the data revealed that most teachers held positive attitude towards errors and error correction. They paid much attention to those errors impeding communication and occurring prevalently in students' speech. In classroom interaction teachers did not over-react upon their students' linguistic errors on the whole.

Wen (2001) pointed out that overconcern with communication of meaning to neglect accuracy of language use would cause some deviant forms to stabilize in learners' interlanguage system, making it difficult to eradicate them. It has been widely accepted that negative feedback is of prime importance to prevent fossilization (Thornbury, 1999). However, it is impractical and detrimental for teachers to treat every student error in the classroom. Therefore, teachers should find an appropriate way to deal with students' errors. One thing worthy of note is that individual students' language proficiency should be taken into account when teachers decide whether to treat student errors. Instruction on language items beyond the students' reach is of no use, as proved by many empirical studies (Ellis, 1984; Mackey, 1995; Ortega and Long, 1997; Mackey and Philp, 1998; Long et al. , 1999; Philp, 2003). Mistimed correction will even have a deleterious effect on students' learning (Allright and Bailey, 1991). When some erroneous expressions are out of the reach of most students, it is not worthwhile to invest much time and effort in error correction. For those deviant forms requiring negative feedback but difficult to assimilate into students' current interlanguage system, teachers can give students systematic explanation later in class or talk with individual students after class. As suggested by the findings of this study, students, especially non-English majors with low proficiency, want the teacher to illustrate the use of English items or structure systematically and offer them opportunities to practice more.

Compared with NEM teachers, EM teachers seemed to treat students' errors less often in class. Given English majors' higher language ability and higher sense of awareness of errors, such corrective behavior was advisable. It could also be seen from the teachers' responses that EM teachers attached more importance to the communicative function of English as a language, while NEM teachers cared more about whether the students could grasp what was required of them by the syllabus or nationwide examinations. It was understandable with regard to different academic focus of English majors and non-English majors.

It was found that that some teachers had taken students' individual differences into account in deciding whether to provide corrective feedback in class. This finding was inspiring because teachers' corrective behavior met the students' needs. A proportion of students, especially students with low proficiency, low self-esteem and low L2 confidence, were fond of individual talks after class and systematic explanations in class. As to introverts, low risk-takers and students with high language anxiety level, they were also in need of error treatment from their teachers. It seems unnecessary for teachers to deliberately ignore some of their errors and correct them less than other students. They will not get hurt if they are provided with positive affective feedback. The distinction made between these students and others will do no good to their study.

Compared with whole-class activities, some teachers treated errors more often in pair/group work, while some provided less negative feedback. It is really the case that we should enable the students to learn to communicate with the second language by involving them in doing pair/group work. However, treating errors on these occasions do not necessarily interrupt the students' communication. As Brumfit (1983) pointed out, teaching should be given at an optimal moment when the students felt the need to improve themselves and when they were most open to noticing the gap. Pair/group work provides the teachers with the opportunities to help individual students to move forward in the development continuum. Error treatment on such occasions is more effective for individual students.

Peer correction is considered to be an important means to help students reformulate their nontargetlike expressions (Bruton and Samuda, 1980; Pica et al. 1996; Zhu, 1996). From students' response to the question concerned with peer correction, it can be seen that students differ in the frequency they provide their peers with corrections. Extroverts, students with high self-esteem, high risk-takers, students with low anxiety level and students with high L2 confidence tended to provide error correction more frequently. Teachers can encourage students, including introverts, students with low self-esteem and low L2 confidence, to correct their peers' errors when they were sure of the correctness of their suggestions. This will not only help improve the quality of student talk, but also generate a sense of responsibility in the students. To assign students to cooperate with different classmates in pair/group work is helpful for their study, since different pattern of cooperation may trigger different behavior from students.

4.3.2   What types of errors were treated

4.3.2.1   Teacher's opinion and corrective behavior

On the basis of review on other researchers' classification of errors and my observation in EFL classrooms, I classified errors into five types: *pronunciation errors*, errors on the accurate pronunciation of vowels and consonants, misplacement of stress or improper use of intonation;

71

grammatical errors, errors resulting from violation of grammatical rules, such as errors on subject and verb agreement, missing-s for plural forms or third person singular verb in present tense and errors on the whole sentence structure; *lexical errors*, errors due to improper use of words or incompletion of words; *expression errors*, errors existing in inappropriate and nonnativelike expressions, though the expressions are well-formed on the surface; and *discourse errors*, errors unable to be understood in the context, though the utterances are not erroneous when analyzed separately.

1) Correction of different types of errors

There was one item concerned with the teachers' correction of different types of errors: "Among all errors in students' speech, you treated _____ most frequently. ① pronunciation errors; ② grammatical errors; ③ lexical errors; ④ expression errors; ⑤ discourse errors. " Analysis of the teachers' response suggested that errors receiving most attention were expression errors. Teachers making this choice accounted for 60% (65% EM teachers and 55% of NEM teachers) of the whole teacher group (see Table 10). Next to this type of errors were grammatical errors and pronunciation errors, which were chosen by 40% (32. 5% of EM teachers; 47. 5% of NEM teachers) and 37. 5% of the teachers (32. 5% of EM teachers; 42. 5% of NEM teachers) respectively. EM teacher group seemed to attach more importance to expression errors, while NEM teacher group tended to put more weight on correction of grammatical errors and pronunciation errors. This could also be inferred from the teachers' response to another item in the questionnaire, in which teachers were required to rank order the five types of errors according to the priority given to them in error treatment. Forty percent of EM teachers and 27. 5% of NEM teachers ranked expression errors as the first. Thirty percent of EM teachers and thirty percent of NEM teachers considered pronunciation errors most important. Twenty percent of EM teachers and ten percent of NEM teachers ranked it the second. Next in the priority list was grammatical errors. More NEM teachers (20%) considered it necessary for this type of errors to receive greatest attention than EM teachers (12.5%).

Table 10   Teachers' treatment of different types of errors

	EM teachers	NEM teachers	Total
Pronunciation errors	13 32.5%	17 42.5%	30 37.5%
Grammatical errors	13 32.5%	19 47.5%	32 40%
Lexical errors	9 22.5%	10 25%	19 23.8%
Expression errors	26 65%	22 55%	48 60%
Discourse errors	1 2.5%	2 5%	3 3.7%

2) Types of errors occurring most frequently in students' speech

To find out the reason why teachers take such corrective behavior, I analyzed their responses to another related item and obtained detailed information in interviews. As to the item concerned with types of errors occurring most often in students' speech, grammatical errors were ranked the first (67.5% of EM teachers and 77.5% of NEM teachers) (see Table 11). Followed were lexical errors (42.5% of EM teachers and 47.5% of NEM teachers), expression errors (40% of EM teachers and 25% of NEM teachers), pronunciation errors (17.5% of EM teachers and 27.5% of NEM teachers) and discourse errors (5% of EM teachers). From the interview it could be perceived that English majors and non-English majors had different problems in language learning. Pronunciation errors of English majors mainly result from occasional misplacement of word stress and inappropriate intonation, while non-

English majors often have trouble with the pronunciation of individual words because of unfamiliarity or lack of necessary linguistic knowledge. Some pronunciation errors committed by non-English majors even twist

Table 11　Errors occurring most frequently in students' speech

	EM teachers	NEM teachers	Total
Pronunciation errors	7 17.5%	11 27.5%	18 22.5%
Grammatical errors	27 67.5%	31 77.5%	58 72.5%
Lexical errors	17 42.5%	19 47.5%	36 45%
Expression errors	16 40%	10 25%	26 32.5%
Discourse errors	2 5%	0	2 2.5%

the meaning of the word, making the whole sentence unable to be understood. Some grammatical errors are made by both English majors and non-English majors, for example, errors resulting from misuse of verb tense. Occurrence of these errors may be caused by anxiety or lack of practice. There are some troublesome grammatical errors in non-English majors' speech that can seldom be found in English majors' interaction, especially those concerned with sentence structure. When non-English majors translate an expression literally from Chinese to English, misordering of sentence constituents may lead to communication failure. Though literal translation is also a problem for English majors, they seldom make the same kind of serious grammatical errors as non-English majors do. Since English majors have wider exposure to the TL, higher language proficiency and a larger repertoire of linguistic items and structures, their utterances cannot be too deviant. As for lexical errors,

74

both English major group and non-English major group are likely to use synonyms improperly under some circumstances. Since English majors realize the importance of enlarging their vocabulary, they like to use new words and expressions regardless of the contexts, which might cause problems in communication. For non-English majors, their difficulty is lack of vocabulary. When they are unable to find the proper word to express their ideas, they misuse a substitute. Thus lexical errors occur. Besides, teachers' responses to the questionnaire also suggested that non-English majors committed grammatical errors and pronunciation errors more often than English majors did. In addition, more EM teachers (40%) reported that expression errors occurred most frequently in their students' speech than NEM teachers (25%). Compared with non-English majors, English majors seemed to make more expression errors.

4.3.2.2 Students' needs and preferences

1) What types of errors should be treated

In the blank filling part of the questionnaire I asked students to rank order five types of errors according to the importance they attached to them as far as error correction was concerned. Results indicated that 36.6% of students (39.8% of EM students and 33.5% of NEM students) put pronunciation errors in the first place and 15.1% of them (12.5% of EM students and 17.6% of NEM students) put this kind of errors in the second. More than one quarter of students (27.3% of EM students and 26.1% of NEM students) gave priority to expression errors. Over 30% of students (30.1% of EM students and 34.7% of NEM students) ranked this type of errors the second. It could be seen that both English majors and non-English majors wanted their teachers to direct considerable attention to these two types of errors. Put next was discourse errors. Nearly twenty percent of students (19.6%) of students thought this type of errors should be treated first. Grammatical errors and lexical errors were ranked fourth and fifth. It could be detected from the detailed information provided by students in the interview that what they cared most was how seriously the errors influenced communication. Take pronunciation errors for example. If the pronunciation of a word was incorrect or inappropriate, misunderstanding or confusion in the part of the interlocutor would arise. As for expression errors, they might cause difficulty in comprehension or become a source of irritation or negative evaluation for native speakers, thus weakening the effect of communication.

2) Correction of what types of errors were most helpful

In the questionnaire there was one question like this: "_____ that the teacher corrected have left deepest impression on me. I would correct them in the future use. ① pronunciation errors; ② grammatical errors; ③ lexical errors; ④ expression errors; ⑤ discourse errors." The results revealed that what impressed EM students most was pronunciation errors corrected by their teachers. Students holding this opinion accounted for 43.2% of the English majors (see Table 12). Next to it was expression errors (27.3% of English majors). As for non-English majors, the expression errors that their teachers treated left greatest impression on them. About thirty percent of the NEM students (30.7%) made the choice. Next were lexical errors (chosen by 23.9% of the students) and grammatical errors (chosen by 21.6% of the NEM students). In contrast to English majors, non-English majors did not have deep impression of pronunciation errors.

Table12 Students opinion:
correction of what types of errors were most helpful

	EM students	NEM students	Total
Pronunciation errors	76 43.2%	33 18.7%	109 31%
Grammatical errors	21 11.9%	38 21.6%	59 16.7%

(Continued Table)

	EM students	NEM students	Total
Lexical errors	28 15.9%	42 23.9%	70 19.9%
Expression errors	48 27.3%	54 30.7%	102 29%
Discourse errors	3 1.7%	9 5.1%	12 3.4%

3) Pair/Group work: what types of errors were treated by peers

When asked what types of errors they usually corrected their peers in doing pair/group work, more than half of the students (56.8% of English majors and 47.2% of non-English majors) chose pronunciation errors (see Table 13). This type of errors seemed to attract most of students' attention when they were engaged in pair work or group work.

Table 13 What types of errors students treated in pair/group work

	EM students	NEM students	Total
Pronunciation errors	100 56.8%	83 47.2%	183 52%
Grammatical errors	62 35.2%	63 35.8%	125 35.5%
Lexical errors	64 36.4%	66 37.5%	130 36.9%
Expression errors	62 35.2%	51 29%	113 32.1%

(Continued Table)

	EM students	NEM students	Total
Discourse errors	8 4.5%	15 8.5%	23 6.5%

Table 14   What types of errors students treated
most in pair work and group work

	EM students	NEM students	Total
Pronunciation errors	77 43.8%	68 38.6%	145 41.2%
Grammatical errors	33 18.7%	38 21.6%	71 20.2%
Lexical errors	39 22.2%	34 19.3%	73 20.7%
Expression errors	37 21%	35 19.9%	72 20.5%
Discourse errors	2 1.1%	8 4.5%	10 2.8%

Students who corrected peers' grammatical errors, lexical errors and expression errors accounted for 35.5%, 36.9% and 32.1% of the whole group respectively. Only twenty-three students (6.5%) reported that they treated peers' discourse errors. To give response to a more detailed question "what I treated most frequently was _____", the students gave similar responses, though the rate of each type of errors decreased according to the request. For the first part of the question, the students could make multiple choices, but for the second part, they could only give one or two answers. One hundred and forty-five students (41.2%) corrected peers' pronunciation errors most often (see Table

78

14). About twenty percent of students provided negative feedback to their peers' grammatical errors, 20.7% of students to their peers' lexical errors and 20.5% of students to their peers' expression errors. In the interview some students told me the reason why they treated their peers' pronunciation errors most. One reason was that this type of errors was the easiest to detect, since improper pronunciation was likely to result in difficulty in comprehension. Another reason was that on treating pronunciation errors, students were confident that their suggestions were correct. When treating other types of errors they were not so sure of the correctness of their negative feedback.

4.3.2.3 Discussion

It was revealed that EM teachers and NEM teachers treated expression errors of students most frequently. Next to them were grammatical errors and pronunciation errors. What the students thought should be put at the top of priority list was pronunciation errors. Followed were expression errors and discourse errors. Though there was disagreement between teachers' corrective behavior and students' expectations, we should not hastily come to the conclusion that teachers' corrective behavior did not meet students' expectations. As mentioned before, teachers had to take many factors into consideration when deciding whether to treat errors. Determination was often made in an instant. Different circumstances see them correct different type of errors. Besides, with regard to the frequent occurrence of grammatical errors, teachers' attention to this type of errors was understandable. Results of this study suggested that EM teachers corrected students' expression errors more than NEM teachers, while NEM teachers corrected students' grammatical errors and pronunciation errors more. This is in conformity with the relatively higher frequency of occurrence of expression errors in EM students' speech and grammatical and pronunciation errors in NEM students' speech.

As was revealed by the results, teachers' correction of pronunciation errors and expression errors left deep impression on English majors. What impressed non-English majors greatly was their teachers' correction of expression errors, lexical errors and grammatical errors. Such findings might provide EM and NEM teachers with valuable information as to what types of errors to correct.

In pair/group work, what students corrected most was their peers' pronunciation errors. They corrected their classmates' grammatical, lexical and expression errors much less often. This might be due to their lack of confidence in pointing out these errors and helping correct them. As to these three types of errors, teachers could motivate students to speak out their opinions on the correctness of the expressions and urge them to find out the proper way of using linguistic items through discussion or consultation of reference books. Students could learn a lot in this course.

4.3.3 How errors were treated

4.3.3.1 Teachers' opinions and corrective behavior

I categorize teachers' negative feedback into six types with reference to the classification made by researchers in previous empirical studies and on the basis of my observation in our EFL classrooms, namely, explicit correction, recast, questioning, elicitation, clarification request and metalinguistic feedback, which is in accordance with the classification of Lyster and Ranta (1997). *Explicit correction* refers to the technique employed by the teacher to attract the students' attention directly to the errors they have made and provided them with the correct forms. The teacher may use such expressions as "Here's a mistake", "That is not acceptable to native speakers", "we cannot say..., we say what?", "You said..., another way of expression may be better..." When giving the correct answer, the teacher may explain or illustrate certain points. *Recast* involves rephrasing of the students' erroneous or inappropriate expressions in a native-like way while the central meaning of the sentences is kept. Upon the occurrence of an error, the teacher may also repeat the devious forms in isolation with a questioning tone. Such negative feedback is *questioning*. On some occasions the teacher may repeat the student's expression with the erroneous part deliberately omitted. He/She may also raise a specific question to help the students realize their errors. These techniques are taken by the teacher to elicit correct forms from the students. They are instances of *elicitation*. Another type of feedback, Examples are "What do you mean by this?" and "Who, who did that?" *Metalinguistic feedback* refers to provision of information related to the well-formedness of the expressions, for instance, "We are talking about something happening in the past, so..." By giving correction in this way, the teacher indicates to the students that there are errors somewhere. The students are to find the errors and correct them by themselves.

Table 15   Frequency of six types of
corrective techniques employed by EM teachers

	Always	**Often**	**Sometimes**	**Rarely**	**Never**
Explicit correction	2 5%	9 22.5%	19 47.5%	10 25%	/
Recast	1 2.5%	22 55%	14 35%	3 7.5%	/
Questioning	1 2.5%	13 32.5%	23 57.5%	3 7.5%	/
Elicitation	1 2.5%	20 50%	16 40%	3 7.5%	/
Clarification request	/	15 37.5%	22 55%	3 7.5%	/
Metalinguistic feedback	/	4 10%	22 55%	11 27.5%	3 7.5%

1) Frequency of corrective techniques employed by the teachers

One item in the questionnaire was about the frequency of corrective techniques employed by the teachers in treating their students' errors. From the number of the teachers who made the choices of "always" and "often" for each type of negative feedback, it can be seen that EM teachers employed recast (2.5% for "always" and 55% for "often") and elicitation (2.5% for "always" and 50% for "often") most frequently (see Table 15). Their use of other types of techniques is clarification request (37.5% for "often"), questioning (2.5% for "always" and 32.5% for "often"), explicit correction (5% for "always" and 22.5% for "often") and metalinguistic feedback (10% for "often"). Similar to EM teachers, NEM teachers also employed recast (37.5% for "often") and elicitation (37.5% for "often") most frequently, but the frequency is much lower compared to EM teacher group (see Table 16). The other types of corrective techniques employed by NEM teachers distributed as follows: explicit feedback (5% for "always" and 30% for "often"), questioning (30% for "often"), clarification request (2.5% for "always" and 17.5% for "often") and metalinguistic feedback (2.5% for "always" and 17.5% for "often"). The results revealed that more EM teachers used the technique of clarification request than NEM teachers, while fewer of them provided explicit correction and metalinguistic feedback than NEM teachers.

Table 16　Frequency of six types of
corrective techniques employed by NEM teachers

	Always	Often	Sometimes	Rarely	Never
Explicit correction	2 5%	12 30%	22 55%	4 10%	/
Recast	/	15 37.5%	21 52.5%	4 10%	/

(Continued Table)

	Always	Often	Sometimes	Rarely	Never
Questioning	/	12 30%	19 47.5%	6 15%	3 7.5%
Elicitation	/	15 37.5%	22 55%	3 7.5%	/
Clarification request	1 2.5%	7 17.5%	25 62.5%	6 15%	1 2.5%
Metalinguistic feedback	1 2.5%	7 17.5%	22 55%	9 22.5%	1 2.5%

2) Most effective way of correction

When asked what they thought was the most effective way of correction, a majority of EM teachers (57.5%) and one half NEM teachers chose "elicitation" (see table 17). According to them, this technique could help the students realize their errors, cause them to think actively and correct errors by themselves, which may serve to solidify the items in their memory. Besides, this type of negative feedback would not hurt the students' feelings. Instead, it would increase their confidence and improve their self-esteem. For similar reasons, 20% of EM teachers regarded questioning as the most effective way of providing negative feedback; 17.5% of EM teachers chose "clarification request". Compared to NEM teachers, EM teachers' attitude toward these two types of feedback was more positive. Altogether only ten percent of NEM teachers viewed questioning and clarification request as the most effective feedback technique. Another difference between EM teacher group and NEM teacher group consisted in their opinions on the effectiveness of explicit correction. Thirty-five percent of NEM teachers considered this technique to be the most effective, but only 12.5% of EM teachers thought so. As some NEM teachers pointed

83

out, since their students did not have very high language level, direct way of correction could provide them with a clear idea as to what expressions were unacceptable so that they could avoid making some errors in later study.

Given the different language proficiency of English majors and non-English majors, the difference in EM teachers' and NEM teachers' opinions was quite understandable. Questioning and clarification request provided the students with opportunities to correct errors by themselves. If the students did not have the ability for self-correction, the corrective behavior would be fruitless. Since English majors were more proficient in language learning, techniques leading to self-repair were more efficient for them. By comparison, explicit correction was more suitable for non-English majors.

Table 17   EM and NEM teachers' opinions on
the most efficient corrective techniques

	EM teachers	NEM teachers	Total
Explicit correction	5 12.5%	14 35%	19 23.7%
Recast	4 10%	4 10%	8 10%
Questioning	8 20%	2 5%	10 12.5%
Elicitation	23 57.5%	20 50%	43 53.8%
Clarification request	7 17.5%	2 5%	9 12.5%
Metalinguistic feedback	1 2.5%	1 2.5%	2 2.5%

3) Different corrective techniques to treat different types of errors

Another item in the blank-filling part of the questionnaire asked the teachers whether they employed different means of correction with regard to different types of errors made by the students and how. An overwhelming majority of the teachers (95% of EM teachers and 97.5% of NEM teachers) gave positive responses. For pronunciation errors, 68.8% of teachers used explicit correction and 23.7% of them employed recast. A few teachers also gave such negative feedback as questioning (10%), elicitation (2.5%) and metalinguistic feedback (3.75%).

Table 18   Techniques employed by teachers to treat grammatical errors

	EM teachers	NEM teachers	Total
Explicit correction	3 7.5%	10 25%	13 16.2%
Recast	18 45%	6 15%	24 30%
Questioning	11 27.5%	12 30%	23 28.8%
Elicitation	8 20%	14 35%	22 27.5%
Clarification request	3 7.5%	6 15%	9 11.2%
Metalinguistic feedback	5 12.5%	10 25%	15 18.7%

Table 19   Techniques employed by teachers to treat lexical errors

	EM teachers	NEM teachers	Total
Explicit correction	10 25%	12 30%	22 27.5%

(Continued Table)

	EM teachers	NEM teachers	Total
Recast	7 17.5%	14 35%	21 26.3%
Questioning	8 20%	10 25%	18 22.5%
Elicitation	12 30%	12 30%	24 30%
Clarification request	7 17.5%	3 7.5%	10 12.5%
Metalinguistic feedback	/	1 2.5%	1 1.2%

As for correction of grammatical errors, there was remarkable difference between EM teacher group and NEM teacher group. The feedback technique employed most frequently by EM teachers was recast (45%), while the means taken by NEM teachers most often was elicitation (35%) (see Table 18). By contrast, recast was only provided by 15% of NEM teachers. Only 20% of EM teachers corrected grammatical errors by elicitation. What's more, explicit correction was provided more by NEM teachers (25%) than by EM teachers (7.5%). The number of NEM teachers who employed metalinguistic feedback to correct students' grammatical errors was twice as many as that of EM teachers.

As to lexical errors, the teachers used such corrective techniques as elicitation, explicit correction, recast and questioning. Comparatively speaking, clarification request and metalinguistic feedback were rarely provided by these teachers (see Table 19). More EM teachers (17.5%) used metalinguistic feedback than NEM teachers (7.5%), while more NEM teachers (35%) preferred to recast the students' erroneous expressions than EM teachers (17. 5%).

With regard to expression errors, 41. 3% of the teachers (45% of EM teachers and 37. 5% of NEM teachers) employed the technique of elicitation; 25% , questioning; 23. 5% , explicit correction; 21. 2% , recast; 16. 2% , clarification request and 5% , metalinguistic feedback (see Table 20). Fewer EM teachers seemed to prefer to use questioning in response to students' expression errors.

Table 20   Techniques employed by teachers to treat expression errors

	EM teachers	NEM teachers	Total
Explicit correction	8 20%	11 27. 5%	19 23. 5%
Recast	7 17. 5%	10 25%	17 21. 2%
Questioning	8 20%	12 30%	20 25%
Elicitation	18 45%	15 37. 5%	33 41. 3%
Clarification request	6 15%	7 17. 5%	13 16. 2%
Metalinguistic feedback	3 7. 5%	1 2. 5%	4 5%

For discourse errors, 36. 3% of the teachers (40% of EM teachers and 32. 5% of NEM teachers) used clarification request, 26. 2% (22. 5 of EM teachers and 30% of NEM teachers) employed elicitation (see Table 21). Other types of feedback were also provided by some

87

teachers: metalinguistic feedback by 15% of the teachers, explicit correction by 12. 5% of the teachers, questioning by 11. 3% of the teachers and recast by 7. 5% of the teachers. It appeared that more NEM teachers tended to provide students with metalinguistic feedback and recast upon the occurrence of students' discourse errors.

Table 21　Techniques employed by teachers to treat discourse errors

	EM teachers	NEM teachers	Total
Explicit correction	6 15%	4 10%	10 12. 5%
Recast	1 2. 5%	5 12. 5%	6 7. 5%
Questioning	6 15%	3 7. 5%	9 11. 3%
Elicitation	9 22. 5%	12 30%	21 26. 2%
Clarification request	16 40%	13 32. 5%	29 36. 3%
Metalinguistic feedback	3 7. 5%	9 22. 5%	12 15%

4) Corrective behavior: attitude and wording

The second open-ended question in the questionnaire was about teachers' attitude and wording when providing students with negative feedback. The teachers stated that they were tolerant of students' errors. They did not scold students for the errors they had made. "I show my respect to my students. I usually talk with them in a friendly tone," said an EM teacher. "I show my sincerity in correction, no sarcasm," an NEM teacher wrote. "I tell my students that everyone errs at some time or other. As a teacher, I will make mistakes myself. I hope they will correct my mistakes," another EM teachers stated. A sense of humor from the teacher seemed to be beneficial sometimes. "For some interesting errors, I will make jokes about them. Instruction integrated with entertainment is effective," suggested by an NEM teacher. Some teachers mentioned that they were not only cautious of the tone they took in correction but also of wording. They would use such expressions as "I'm afraid. . . ", "It seems to me that. . . ", "Are you sure it is. . . ", "Why not try to use. . . ", "It would be better if you. . . " and "Would you please say. . . in this way?" to make corrections more acceptable to their students.

5) Corrective techniques employed with regard to students' individual differences

As mentioned before, there was an item about teachers' corrective behavior to students with different proficiency, gender, characteristics, language anxiety and L2 confidence. When teacher were asked whether their corrective behavior was different when the students belonged to the following groups: ① extroverts or introverts; ② male students or female students; ③ HP students or LP students; ④ students with high self-esteem or students with low self-esteem; ⑤ high risk-takers or low risk-takers; ⑥ students with high level of language anxiety or students with low level of language anxiety, it was found that only gender of the students did not result in much difference in teachers' corrective behavior. Only 27. 5% of teachers (25% of EM teachers and 30% of NEM teachers) stated that they corrected male students and female students differently. They would use more explicit correction to male students, since correction in public was supposed to be more acceptable to male students. These teachers reported that they would provide female students with implicit negative feedback, to help them perceive their errors and make correction. A great majority of teachers did not think it necessary to make a distinction between male student group and female student group in providing negative feedback.

For extroverts and introverts, 77. 5% of the teachers (67. 5% of EM teachers and 87. 5% of NEM teachers) adopted different techniques in providing negative feedback. When the error producers were extroverts, teachers tended to give explicit feedback or pointed out errors immediately for themselves to self-correct. For introverts, teachers tended to use recast or provide them with clear and specific clues in the tone of statements or questions.

As to students with different language proficiency, 77. 5% of the teachers (62. 5% of EM teachers and 92. 5% of NEM teachers) reported different ways of corrections. When the error producers were HP students, some teachers employed explicit correction more, since these students usually had high self-esteem and they would not feel discouraged on receiving negative feedback. Some teachers often used recast because HP students were supposed to have a higher sense of awareness of errors and they were likely to notice the discrepancy between teachers' expressions and their own. Some teachers also regarded it a good way to use such corrective techniques as metalinguistic feedback to allow HP students for self-correction. As for LP students, some teachers preferred to use such implicit corrective techniques as recast to treat these students' errors in order not to make LP students feel embarrassed or lose face. Some teachers gave LP students more encouragement and provided them with more detailed clues to help them to find and correct their errors. Some teachers also preferred to point out LP students' errors and told them the correct way of expressions directly. According to these teachers, LP students were not supposed to be able to correct their own errors. These students might not be able to detect teachers' implicit corrective feedback.

A large proportion of teachers (65% of EM teachers and 92. 5% of NEM teachers) also treated students with high self-esteem and students with low self-esteem in different ways. For students with high self-esteem, teachers usually employed such means as questioning or elicitation to help them detect their errors and self-repair. Explicit correction was also used on some occasions. For students with low self-esteem, teachers tended to recast their erroneous expressions or correct them after expressing their appreciation of these students' contributions. A few teachers also offered more opportunities to these students to repeat the correct expressions or practice what had been learned.

Most NEM teachers (62. 5%) and less than half of EM teachers (42. 5%) reported that the risk-taking level of the students was the factor they took into consideration in providing negative feedback. They would correct high risk-takers explicitly and low risk-takers implicitly. High risk-takers were not likely to get frustrated from explicit correction, while low risk-takers, mostly introverts, would find implicit correction more acceptable.

With regard to students' level of language anxiety, 72. 5% of EM teachers and 82. 5% of NEM teachers corrected errors made by students with high level of anxiety and students with low level of anxiety differently. For students with high level of anxiety, teachers tended to correct them less in class and used such implicit corrective techniques as recast to treat their errors. For students with low level of anxiety, teachers would let them know their errors immediately and use questioning or elicitation to trigger them to make modifications to their expressions.

It could be seen from the findings that students' individual differences had more effect on NEM teachers' corrective behavior. Comparatively, fewer EM teachers provided different corrective techniques to students with different language proficiency and characteristics.

6) Non-verbal means of correction

The third open-ended question in teacher's questionnaire was to examine whether teachers employed non-verbal means in error treatment and whether they thought such means were effective. A substantial proportion of the teachers (77. 5% of EM teachers and 72. 5% of NEM teachers) reported that they did use such non-verbal means as facial expression, gestures and body language when errors occurred in their students' speech. Frowns expressions of puzzle, surprise, questioning or unexpectedness, stares, widened eyes and head shakes were employed by some teachers. Most teachers viewed non-verbal means as effective. As one NEM students stated, such means could kill two birds with one stone: students could realize their errors and correct them without interrupting the flow of thought. At the same time, students would not get hurt when receiving negative feedback in front of the whole class. What's more, non-verbal means could help make the classroom atmosphere relaxing and motivating.

Though effectiveness of non-verbal means gained much approval from the teachers, it was suggested that one should be cautious of their use. According to some teachers, LP students might have difficulty correcting their own errors. It was of little use for them only to realize the existence of errors in speech, since they had no idea where the errors were located and what were the proper ways to express their ideas. Besides, there were times that students did not look at their teachers when answering questions in class. In that case it was impossible for these students to notice the teachers' non-verbal behavior. Compared with verbal feedback, non-verbal means were not explicit enough to ensure noticing. Teachers held the opinion that verbal means of correction were more effective under some circumstances.

7) How often teachers let students' peers correct their errors in whole-class activities

Table 22   How often the teachers asked students' peers to correct their errors

	EM teachers	NEM teachers	Total
Always	/	/	/
Often	4 10%	2 5%	6 7.5%
Sometimes	19 47.5%	21 52.5%	40 50%
Rarely	13 32.5%	13 32.5%	26 32.5%
Never	4 10%	4 10%	8 10%

After deciding to treat the students' errors, the teachers can provide the correct answers by themselves, to transfer the responsibility to other students or allow the students to make self-repair. When asked how often they required other students to help correct the errors, 7.5% of the teachers chose "often", half of the teachers chose "sometimes", 32.5% chose "rarely" and 10% chose "never" (see Table 22). There was not noticeable difference between EM teacher group and NEM teacher group. Those teachers who developed a positive attitude toward peer correction in teacher-fronted activities regarded this as an effective means to involve more students in the learning process, to heighten more students' awareness of errors, to help students activate their interlanguage system to solve linguistic problems and to create an atmosphere of harmony and warmth in the classroom. These teachers considered peer correction in whole-class activities to be beneficial to both the error makers and their peers who made attempts to correct errors. For error makers, they would find it more acceptable to be corrected by peers who were at an equal position with them. The level of anxiety would be lower. The correct forms offered by peers would also leave a deep impression on them. For those students who help correcting peers' errors, their linguistic knowledge would be solidified.

Some teachers stated in their responses that they rarely or never transferred the responsibility of correcting errors to students' peers because this might put pressure on the error makers and destroy their confidence. These students might infer from teachers' behavior that they were inferior to their peers. They would feel frustrated. Another factor accounting for some teachers' reluctance to let students' peers correct errors was that peer correction took more time in class than other ways of correction.

8) What kind of students teachers tended to offer opportunities for self-repair

As analyzed above, the techniques leading to self-repair or peer repair, such as questioning, elicitation, clarification request and metalinguistic feedback, were sometimes employed by teachers. Therefore, in the blank filling part of the questionnaire I asked the teachers to make choices as to what kind of students they tended to offer the opportunities for self-correction. The first group included ① extroverts; ② introverts; ③ both. Fifteen EM teachers (37.5%) and nineteen NEM teachers (47.5%) declared that they tended to let extroverted students correct their own errors. Sixty percent of EM teachers and half of NEM teachers stated that they would allow both extroverts and introverts to do so. Only one EM teacher and one NEM teacher said that they let introverts self-repair. The second group included students of different gender: ① male students; ② female students; ③ both. It seemed that gender of the students had little effect on the teachers' corrective behavior. A substantial proportion of teachers (90% of EM teachers and 92.5% of NEM teachers) made the third choice: both. The third group was students with different language proficiency: ① students with high proficiency; ② students with low proficiency; ③ all the students regardless of their language proficiency. Fifteen EM teachers (37.5%)

and 20 NEM teachers (50%) stated that they would allow students with high proficiency to correct errors by themselves. Twenty-five EM teachers (62.5%) and twenty NEM teachers (50%) declared students' language level would not influence their decision on offering opportunities to students for self-correction. Compared with EM teacher group, NEM teacher group seemed to care more about the students' language ability. The fourth group was students with different level of self-esteem: ① students with high level of self-esteem; ② students with low level of self-esteem; ③ all the students regardless of their level of self-esteem. Eighteen EM teachers (45%) and twenty NEM teachers (50%) declared that they would let students with high self-esteem correct errors by themselves. Twenty-one EM teachers (52.5%) and seventeen NEM teachers (42.5%) stated that students' self-esteem level did not count much in their correction. The fifth group was about students' level of risk-taking: ① high risk-takers; ② low risk-takers; ③ all the students regardless of their risk-taking level. There was noticeable inconformity between EM teacher group and NEM teacher group in their responses to this part of the question. More NEM teachers (50%) tended to offer more opportunities to high risk-takers for self-repair than EM teachers (37.5%). EM teachers appeared to pay less attention to the risk-taking level of students than NEM teachers. The last part of the question was about the anxiety level of the students: ① students who are very anxious when speaking; ② students that do not feel anxious when speaking; ③ all the students regardless of their anxiety level. More NEM teachers (60%) stated that they tended to let those students who did not feel anxious to correct errors by themselves. Nineteen EM teachers (47.5%) behaved in the same way. Students' anxiety level seemed to be less important to EM teachers on decision making than NEM teachers. Nineteen EM teachers (47.5%) declared that they would allow students to self-correct regardless of their anxiety level. Only eleven NEM teachers (27.5%) made the same statement.

On the whole, it could be seen that NEM teachers considered students' individual differences more often than EM teachers in deciding whether to allow students for self-repair. Students' personality and language proficiency were both taken into account.

9) When teachers corrected errors

There was one question eliciting when the teachers treated student errors: "Upon the occurrence of errors in your students' speech, when do you usually treat their errors? ① correct immediately; ② correct after the completion of a sentence; ③ correct after the student finished with the expression; ④ correct after class; ⑤ correct later". The results suggested that an overwhelming majority of teachers (85% of EM teachers and 82.5% of NEM teachers) corrected errors after the students finished with their expression (see Table 23). According to these teachers, this way of correction would urge students to restructure their linguistic system towards more accuracy and increase their sensitivity to errors. The erroneous expressions receiving feedback served as negative evidences to prevent the recurrence of the same errors.

Table 23　When teachers treated students' errors

	EM teachers	NEM teachers	Total
Immediately	/	1 2.5%	1 1.3%
Upon completion of a sentence	3 7.5%	3 7.5%	6 7.5%
Upon completion of the expression	34 85%	33 82.5%	67 83.8%
After class	3 7.5%	1 2.5%	4 5%
Later	/	2 5%	2 2.5%

Meanwhile such corrective behavior would not break students' flow of thought, destroy their confidence, or increase their anxiety. Besides, there was time and opportunity for students to reflect upon the mistakes they had made and corrected them by themselves. Analysis of teachers' responses also suggested that a few teachers preferred to treat students' errors upon their completion of a sentence. They thought it necessary to do so because the existence of the errors might influence message comprehension without timely treatment. Moreover, the instant correction would be beneficial to students for their interlanguage development. The only one NEM teacher who chose "correct immediately" explained that some errors, especially pronunciation errors, would result in misunderstanding or difficulty in comprehension. That was why such problems should be dealt with immediately. Four teachers reported that they preferred to treat errors after class. In their opinion, error correction was an indication of negative evaluation. To treat errors after class by talking with individual students could protect the students from being hurt and maintain their self-esteem. One female EM teacher pointed out that introverted students required such treatment especially. Another two teachers wrote on the questionnaire that they did not like to make immediate corrections but to treat errors some time later. In their opinions, the development of fluency in students' speech should be valued over accuracy for the time being. Frequent treatment of errors in class would discourage students from making further attempts to use English.

10) How errors were treated in student-centered pair/group work

As mentioned before, 52.5% of EM teachers and 77.5% of NEM teachers reported that their corrective behavior was not the same in whole class activities and pair/group work. Some teachers tended to recast students' errors in whole class activities and correct errors more explicitly when the students were doing pair/group work. When the students exchanged ideas in pairs or small groups, the atmosphere was relaxing. They would not be threatened with losing face when receiving negative

97

feedback. For some teachers, the time taken out for correction was the factor that influenced their corrective behavior. Some teachers would choose corrective techniques that took little time in whole class activities, but they would employ more time-consuming means such as clarification request, elicitation and questioning in pair/group work. They tended to provide the correct answers directly in teacher-centered activities, but allow students to self-correct in student-centered pair/group work.

4.3.3.2 Students' needs and preferences

1) Preferred corrective techniques employed by the teachers

There was one question about students' preferred way of error treatment, which was like this: "I prefer the teacher to use this technique to correct my errors in class: _____ ① correct explicitly; ② recast; ③ give hints and allow me to correct by myself." The students were allowed to make one or two choices in response to this question. More than sixty percent of the students wanted their teachers to give them hints and enabled them to correct errors by themselves (see Table 24). More English majors (65.3%) had such a request than non-English majors (56.3%). More than one third of the students found explicit correction and recast to be good ways of error treatment for them.

Table 24　Students' preferences on
corrective techniques employed by the teacher

	EM students	NEM students	Total
To correct explicitly	72 40.9%	61 34.7%	133 37.8%
To recast	61 34.7%	62 35.2%	123 34.9%
To give hints to trigger self-repair	115 65.3%	99 56.3%	214 60.8%

98

Distinction could be found among students with different language proficiency and personality in their preferences for teachers' corrective techniques. It seemed that HP students, extroverts, students with high self-esteem, high risk-takers and students with high L2 confidence were more fond of being given hints for self-repair when compared with LP students, introverts, students with low self-esteem, low risk-takers and students with low L2 confidence. Students having such a preference included 70.3% HP students, 57.4% LP students, 65.9% of extroverts, 51.3% of introverts, 64.3% of students with high self-esteem, 54.2% of students with low self-esteem, 66.7% of high risk-takers, 40.3% of low risk-takers, 61.8% of students with high L2 confidence and 46.6% of students with low L2 confidence. Besides, more LP students (42.6%), low risk-takers (46.8%), students with high level of language anxiety (38.4%) and students with low L2 confidence (41.4%) were in favor of recast than HP students (25.7%), high risk-takers (25%), students with low level of language anxiety (28.3%) and students with high L2 confidence (26.5%). The preferences of LP students were distributed like this: to give hints for self-repair (57.4%), to recast (42.6%) and to correct explicitly (40.7%). For extroverts, the students who favored self-repair (65.9%) were almost twice as many as those who liked explicit correction (33.3%) or recast (33.3%). The distribution pattern of low risk-takers' preferences was like this: to recast (46.8%), to give hints for self-repair (40.3%) and to correct explicitly (37.1%). The preferences of other student group, including HP student group, introvert group, students with low self-esteem, students with high self-esteem, high risk-takers, students with low level of language anxiety, students with high level of language anxiety, students with low L2 confidence and students with high L2 confidence, all distributed in the same order: to give hints for self-repair, to correct explicitly and to recast.

2) Most effective corrective techniques taken by the teachers

Another item in the questionnaire was to find out what technique the students thought was the most effective one for them. It could be seen from Table 25 that to provide hints and allow students to self-correct was viewed as the most effective for more than half of the students (52.3% of English majors and 48.3% of non-English majors). Recast was considered to be most effective by 28.7% of the students. About 20% of the students found explicit correction most effective for them.

Table 25　Most effective corrective techniques for the students

	EM students	NEM students	Total
To correct explicitly	33 18.7%	41 23.3%	74 21%
To recast	51 29%	50 28.4%	101 28.7%
To give hints to trigger self-repair	92 52.3%	85 48.3%	177 50.3%

When further analysis was made, it was found that different corrective techniques appealed to students with different proficiency and characteristics. For five groups, namely, extrovert group, students with low self-esteem, high risk-taker group, students with high language anxiety level and students with low L2 confidence, the most effective feedback technique distributed in decreasing order like this: to give hints for self-repair, to recast and to correct explicitly. For HP students and students with high L2 confidence, explicit correction and recast were of equal effectiveness for them. Their favorite also was to give hints for self-repair. Students in these two groups who considered hints for self-repair to most effective (56.8% of HP students; 53% of students with high L2 confidence) were more than twice as many as those who preferred recast or explicit correction (21.6% of HP students; 23.5% of students with high L2 confidence). Giving hints for self-repair was

100

also most frequently chosen as the most effective means of correction by students in introvert group (46. 3%) , students with high self-esteem (52. 4%) and students with low language anxiety level (50. 9%). As for the other two corrective techniques, more students in these three groups considered explicit correction to be effective than recast. Students who thought explicit correction to be the most effective included 31. 3% of introverts, 28. 6% of students with high self-esteem and 28. 3% of students with low language anxiety level, while students in fond of recast accounted for 22. 5% of introverts, 19% of students with high self-esteem and 20. 8% of students with low language anxiety level. For LP students and low risk-takers, recast was the most appealing technique employed by their teachers. Students holding this opinion accounted for 42. 6% of LP students and 43. 6% of low risk-takers. Next to recast was giving hints for self-correction (37% of LP students and 38. 7% of low risk-takers). Explicit correction was considered to be most effective only by 20. 4% of LP students and 17. 7% of low risk-takers.

Marked differences could be detected between HP students and LP students, extroverts and introverts, high risk-takers and low risk-takers, students with high language anxiety level and students with low language anxiety level and students with high L2 confidence and students with low L2 confidence. Giving hints for self-repair was found to be effective to more HP students (56. 8%) , more extroverts (57. 1%) , more high risk-takers (58. 3%) and more students with high L2 confidence (53%) than LP students (37%) , introverts (46.3%) , low risk-takers (38. 7%) and students with low L2 confidence (43. 1%). More LP students (42. 6%) , more low risk-takers (43. 6%) and more students with high language anxiety level (35. 6%) viewed recast as the most effective means of correction than HP students (21. 6%) , high risk-takers (27. 1%) and students with low language anxiety level (20.8%).

· 3) Who to correct errors

When asked who they wanted to correct their errors, the teacher, peers or themselves, 66. 2% of the students (64. 2% of EM students and 68. 2% of NEM students) responded that they thought the teacher was most suitable to provide regative feedback (see Table 26). In their opinions, teachers were "authorities" in English, and so their corrections

Table 26   Students' opinion on whom they like to correct errors

	EM students	NEM students	Total
Teacher	113 64. 2%	120 68. 2%	233 66. 2%
Peers	75 42. 6%	72 40. 9%	147 41. 8%
Self	110 62. 5%	91 51. 7%	201 57. 1%

Table 27   Students' opinion on whom they like best to correct errors

	EM students	NEM students	Total
Teacher	73 41. 5%	83 47. 2%	156 44. 3%
Peers	10 5. 7%	15 8. 5%	25 7. 1%
Self	93 52. 8%	78 44. 3%	171 48. 6%

were convincing. More than half of the students (57. 1%) also wanted the opportunities to correct errors by themselves. More English majors (62. 5%) preferred self-correction than non-English majors (51. 7%). According to some students, self-correction would cause them to think and might leave deep impression on them. Another reason was that self-correction was a good way of making up for the commitment of errors and saving face. It could also be seen that 41.8% of students also wanted their peers to help correct their errors. As some students mentioned in the interview, correction from peers were acceptable to them. That could also be helpful to them in learning. "As long as what they said was correct, I would accept pleasantly," said one English major. However, there were also many students who held different opinions. "I don't want my classmates to correct my errors. The teacher can correct my errors directly. If he asks other students to correct my errors, it means I'm inferior to others," one non-English major said. "My classmates don't know much more than me. They may not be able to correct my errors. At last the teacher still has to correct them by herself. It's a waste of time," another non-English major stated. When asked whom they liked best to correct their errors, 48.6% of the students (52.8% of English majors and 44.3% of non-English majors) preferred to self-correct their errors (see Table 27). More than 40% of the students (41.5% of EM students and 47.2% of NEM students) wanted their teachers to correct their errors. Only 7.1% of them (5.7% of English majors and 8.5% of non-English majors) wanted peers to correct errors for them. It was suggested that English majors were more fond of self-correction than non-English majors. This might have something to do with English majors' higher language competence. They were more capable of correcting their errors with the necessary help from their teachers.

4) When the teacher should correct errors

In response to the question "With regard to errors in my speech, I want my teacher to _____. ① correct them immediately; ② correct them after I finish with the sentence; ③ correct them after I finish with my expression; ④ correct them after class; ⑤ correct them later", a majority of the students (72.4%) wanted their teachers to correct errors after they finished expressing their ideas (see Table 28). Students wanting immediate error treatment account for 10. 5% of all the subjects. Fifteen percent of the students think that the teacher should treat errors upon completion of a sentence.

Table 28　Students' opinions on when the teacher should treat their errors

	EM students	NEM students	Total
Immediately	18 10. 2%	19 10. 8%	37 10. 5%
Upon completion of a sentence	26 14. 8%	27 15. 4%	53 15%
Upon completion of the expression	127 72. 2%	128 72. 7%	255 72. 4%
After class	5 2. 8%	2 1. 1%	7 2%
Later	/	/	/

Though all the student groups were similar in that a substantial proportion of students wanted the teachers to treat their errors after they finished with expression, there were noticeable differences among different student groups. Distinction could be seen between HP student group and LP student group and extrovert and introvert group. About twenty percent of LP students (20.4%) wanted their teachers to correct errors upon their completion of sentences, while only 6. 8% of HP students were in favor of such error treatment. In English major group, more extroverts (21.1%) preferred immediate correction than introverts (4.7%). In non-English major group, more extroverts (26.1%) were in favor of error treatment upon completion of sentences than introverts (5.4%), while more introverts (78.4%) were fond of correction upon completion of expressions than extroverts (65.2%).

5) What students thought their teachers' attitude and wording

104

should be like in treating errors

When asked whether they cared about their teachers' attitude and wording in providing negative feedback, some students responded that they did not since the teachers' purpose was to help them with their study. However, most students expressed their concern about the teachers' attitude and wording. They hoped their teachers could be sincere, friendly and patient. "To improve spoken English, (building up) confidence is most important," a non-English major stated. Some students wanted their teachers to point out their errors directly without talking in a roundabout way, spending a lot of time in correction and making them feel ashamed of their "misdoings". Some students expressed the hope that teachers could discuss with them about their errors like a friend, not as an authority who was in a much higher position.

6) Reaction to teachers' non-verbal means of correction

There was an open-ended question in the questionnaire asking the students whether they had noticed the non-verbal means of correction taken by their teachers and what were their opinions on that. Some students responded that they did not notice. According to them, they were not used to looking at teachers in the face when they spoke English in class. Some said they were short-sighted and could not see teacher's face clearly. Some explained that they were not sensitive enough to detect the meaning in teachers' nonverbal behavior. An NEM LP student stated that he could realize there was something wrong through his teacher's facial expression, but he did not know where the error was. There were also a large number of students who found their teachers' eye contact and facial expressions effective. According to them, a look of surprise or a frown in the part of the teacher would enable them to beware the occurrence of errors. They could make reformulation accordingly.

7) Attitude towards teachers' different corrective behavior in whole-

class activity and pair/group work

There was one question in the questionnaire asking students whether they thought it acceptable for the teachers to take different means of correction in whole-class activities and pair/group work. It turned out that an overwhelming majority of students (90. 9% English majors and 90. 3% non-English majors) approved of this. Highly aware of the significance of error correction, a wealth of students explained that they did not care much about the techniques employed by their teachers as long as the teachers' corrective behavior could help them improve. Many said that when they were engaged in pair work or group discussion, communication was natural and there was not great concern about losing face. Besides, the distance between them and the teacher was shorter. Therefore, negative feedback provided by the teachers was more acceptable, whether the corrections were direct or not. Some students also pointed out that it was advisable for teachers to treat errors in different ways under different circumstances with regard to students' needs.

8) Corrective techniques employed by students in pair work and group work

An item in the blank-filling part of the questionnaire went like this: "When I treat my peers' errors, I usually use such a technique/ techniques _____ . ① to correct explicitly; ② to recast; ③ to give hints to enable them to self-correct. Students making the first, second and third choice took up 40. 3% , 50. 9% and 21. 9% of the whole student group respectively (see Table 29). Recast appeared to be the most frequent measure taken by students in peer correction. Though the difference between EM student group and NEM student group was not very impressive, it could be detected that more English majors tended to allow their peers to self-repair rather than provide the correct answers directly. Students making the third choice accounted for 25. 6% of English majors and 18. 2% of non-English majors. This might have something to do with English majors' higher language ability. Compared with non-English majors, EM student group was more capable of correcting their linguistic errors.

Table 29   Corrective techniques employed by students in peer correction

	EM students	NEM students	Total
To correct explicitly	69 39.2%	73 41.5%	142 40.3%
To recast	88 50%	91 51.7%	179 50.9%
To give hints to trigger self-repair	45 25.6%	32 18.2%	77 21.9%

When individual differences were taken into account, it seemed that HP students, extroverts, students with high self-esteem, high risk-takers, students with low language anxiety level and those with high L2 confidence liked to give hints to their peers to enable them to self-repair. Students who corrected peers in this way include 56.8% of HP students, 37% of LP students, 35.7% of extroverts, 25% of introverts, 29.8% of students with high self-esteem, 12.5% of students with low self-esteem, 27.1% of high risk-takers, 17.7% of low risk-takers, 28.3% of students with low language anxiety level, 12.3% of students with high language anxiety level, 26.5% of students with high L2 confidence and 8.6% of students with low L2 confidence. LP students and students with low self-esteem were more fond of recasting their peers' errors. Students providing this type of negative feedback accounted for 42.6% of LP students, 21.6% of HP students, 56.3% of students with low self-esteem and 41.7% of students with high self-esteem. Low risk-takers and students with low L2 confidence preferred to give explicit correction more. Among students who took such corrective means, there

107

were 41.9% of low risk-takers, 31.3% of high risk-takers, 51.7% of students with low L2 confidence and 38.2% of students with high L2 confidence.

9) To what extent students could perceive their peers' correction

As to the question "When I correct my classmates' errors, they can _____ detect my correction. ① always; ② often; ③ sometimes; ④ rarely; ⑤ never", 18.5% of the students responded that their peers could always realize the correction. A majority of the students (67.9%) found that their peers often had a sense of awareness when their errors were corrected. About sixteen percent of the students said that their peers could sometimes realize their corrective behavior. According to these students, on some occasions the speakers might be so preoccupied with what they wanted to say that they failed to notice what others suggested to them. Besides, some students might pay little attention to the language they use and their peers' responses in doing pair/group work. Therefore, their peers' corrective behavior was often ignored. "A few classmates of mine are quite relaxed (in doing pair or group work). They don't mind whether there are errors in their speech. They just get themselves across. That's OK," an English major said.

10) Peers' corrective techniques preferred by students in doing pair/group work

In response to the question "The corrective technique(s) I want my peers to employ is (are) _____ ① to correct explicitly; ② to recast; ③ to give hints to trigger self-repair", 45.7% of the students chose "to recast", 39.8% of them chose "to correct explicitly" and 32.1% chose "to give hints to trigger self-repair" (see Table 30). Compared with the data we obtained for the question how peers corrected errors, it could be seen that students held a positive attitude towards error treatment enabling self-repair to take place and more students were in need of such correction.

Table 30 Peers' corrective techniques preferred by
students in pair work and group work

	EM students	NEM students	Total
To correct explicitly	68 38.6%	72 40.9%	140 39.8%
To recast	81 46%	80 45.5%	161 45.7%
To give hints to trigger self-repair	62 35.2%	51 29%	113 32.1%

LP students and HP students differed markedly in their preferred
way of peer correction. The favorite corrective technique of LP students
was recast. A majority of LP students (55.6%) made this choice,
while only 32.4% of HP students did so. HP students' wanted their
pairs to give them hints to enable them to self-repair most. Students
preferring self-repair accounted for 44.6% of HP student group, but
only 27.8% of LP student group. Discrepancy also exists between
extrovert student group and introvert student group. More introverts
(47.5%) were fond of explicit correction from peers than extroverts
(31%), while more extroverts (42.9%) longed for the opportunities to
correct errors by themselves than introverts (31.3%). As for low risk-
takers and high risk-takers, both groups preferred recast most (48.4%
of low risk-takers and 47.9% of high risk-takers), and explicit
correction (43.5% of low risk-takers and 37.5% of high risk-takers)
next to it. Nevertheless, more high risk-takers (37.5%) wanted their
peers to give them hints for self-repair than low risk-takers (25.8%).
There was also mismatch in the responses given by students with different
level of language anxiety. More students with high language anxiety level
(50.7%) preferred their peers to recast their erroneous expressions than
students with low language anxiety level (39.6%). The favorite way of

peer correction for students of high language anxiety level was recast, but for students of low language anxiety level, their favorite was explicit correction. With regard to L2 confidence of the students, students with low L2 confidence differed from those with high L2 confidence in that they were fond of explicit correction more. Students who were in favor of explicit correction took up 53.4% of students with low L2 confidence, but only 35.3% of students with high L2 confidence. The favorite way of peer correction for students with low L2 confidence was explicit correction, while that for students with high L2 confidence was recast.

11) Who to provide corrective feedback in pair/group work

There was an item in the questionnaire like this: "In pair work or group work, you will find errors corrected by some classmates more acceptable. Who are they? Please make a choice in each group of answers." The choices were concerned with four aspects: students' language proficiency, personality, gender and familiarity.

a) Language proficiency

A substantial proportion of students (85.5%) found errors corrected by those who had higher language proficiency more acceptable, including 84.1% of English majors and 86.9% of non-English majors. According to these students, their peers having higher language proficiency were more likely to provide correct answers and their feedback was more convincing. More than 10% of students (15.9% of English majors and 11.9% of non-English majors) wanted errors to be treated by those who were at similar language level as them. As two students stated in the interview, the corrections made by their classmates with lower English level might be incorrect. They did not want to follow the suggestions. On the other hand, when their peers with higher language level corrected their errors, they felt inequality and pressure. That's why they would like to cooperate with peers who were on an equal footing with them in English and have their errors corrected by such peers. Students with different language proficiency, personality, anxiety level and L2 confidence showed consistency in their preference for correction by partners with higher language level. For high risk-taker group and low risk-taker group, a substantial proportion of students (91.7% of English majors and 80.6% of non-English majors) also had the same preference. The distinction between these two groups consisted in that low risk-takers were fond of correction from peers with similar language proficiency (19.4%) outnumbered high risk-takers (6.2%).

b) Personality: extrovert or introvert

As far as peers' personality is concerned, about twenty percent of students (21% of English majors and 23.9% of non-English majors) found errors corrected by extroverts more acceptable. In their opinion, extroverts were easy to get along with. When extroverts pointed out errors for them, they would not feel anxious or embarrassed. For the majority of students (76.2% of English majors and 72.1% of non-English majors), they did not care much about the personality of their peers in error treatment. As to those students who favored introverts to correct errors for them, they thought introverts' corrections had high possibility of being correct. "Introverts are quiet most of the time. When they point out errors, they are usually sure of the correctness of their suggestions. They are sincere. I pay much attention to the corrections they make," a non-English major said.

For English majors in extrovert/introvert group, more extroverts were fond of being corrected by extroverts. The students making the choice of "extroverts" took up 36.8% of extroverts among English majors, but only 20.9% of introverts among English majors. As to non-English majors in risk-taking group, a subtle difference consisted in that more low risk-takers (28.6%) seemed to be fond of being corrected by extroverts than high risk-takers (18.2%).

c) Gender: same sex or opposite sex

When asked whether the gender of peers would influence their acceptability of peer correction, an overwhelming majority of students

111

(92. 6% of English majors and 83% of non-English majors) responded that they did not care much about that. Those who wanted peers of the same sex to correct errors accounted for 5. 7% of the students, including 4. 6% of English majors and 6. 8% of non-English majors. They thought they would feel at ease in that case. Twenty-three students (6. 5% of the students), including five English majors and eighteen non-English majors, preferred peers of the opposite sex to correct their errors. According to them, there were scant opportunities to be corrected by such peers. Therefore, their corrections should be taken sincerely and seriously.

There was discrepancy between extroverts and introverts in NEM student group. More than 15% percent of introverts stated that they preferred to have their errors corrected by peers of the same sex, while no extroverts made the same statement. They seemed not to care much about the gender of their peers. In addition, students with low L2 confidence differed from students with high L2 confidence in that more students with low L2 confidence (12. 1%) wanted their errors to be corrected by peers of the same sex. Students having such preference included 12. 1% of students with low L2 confidence, but 1. 5% of students with high L2 confidence.

d) Familiarity

As for the question concerned with the familiarity between the students and their peers, 24. 7% of students (23. 3% of English majors and 26. 1% of non-English majors) responded that they found error treatment from familiar persons more acceptable. A majority of students (73%) did not think the familiarity between them and their peers counted much in error treatment. Only eight students (2. 3% of the students) said that they preferred their errors to be treated by those whom they were unfamiliar with.

More low achievers (37%) and low risk-takers (35. 5%) wanted negative feedback from familiar persons than high achievers (20. 3%)

and high risk-takers (20.8%). Introverts in English major group were more concerned with familiarity of peers. English majors who were fond of error treatment from familiar persons take up 25.6% of introverts and 15.8% of extroverts. Besides, more students with high anxiety level (28.8%) and low L2 confidence (31%) wanted their errors to be corrected by peers they were familiar with than students with low anxiety level (17%) and high L2 confidence (17.6%).

4.3.3.3   Discussion

Analysis of the data revealed that two corrective techniques employed most frequently by teachers were recast and elicitation. EM teachers tended to use clarification request more often than NEM teachers. For students, especially English majors, they preferred corrective techniques enabling them to correct errors by themselves.

Uptake, a term used to describe the learners' responses to feedback following a nontargetlike expressions, has attracted abundant attention. Its contribution to language learning has been realized (Ellis et al., 2001). Such means of negotiation as elicitation and clarification request have been found to be more likely to lead to uptake (Lyster and Ranta, 1997; Loewen, 2004). These feedback techniques push the learners reformulate their expressions and help autonomize already internalized linguistic knowledge so as to result in interlanguage restructuring and enhanced learning (Nobuyoshi and Ellis, 1993; Donato, 1994; Gass and Varonis, 1994; Swain, 1995; de Bot, 1996; Izumi and Bigelow, 2000; Oliver, 2000). Uptake is also a reflection suggesting that the mismatch between the learners' output and the targetlike expressions has been noticed. As Schimidt (1990, 1993, 1994) pointed out, noticing is necessary and essential for learning to take place. Noticing of feedback was considered to associate with L2 learning (Mackey, 2000; Williams, 2001). Though recast was found to be effective on some occasions (Schmidt and Frota, 1986; Oliver, 1995; Izumi, 1998; Long et al., 1998), it can be seen that this feedback technique does not

113

involve learners in as much processing as other output-eliciting techniques do. It is not an effective means to generate noticing. It does not indicate to the learners that modifications are significant (Netten, 1991). That is why in language classrooms recast are sometimes confused with noncorrective repetitions and alternative ways of expressions. In addition, recast denies the students opportunities for self-repair, which is "an important learning activity" (van Lier, 1988: 211) beneficial to interlanguage development and a good way which is more likely to improve learners' ability to monitor their speech (Chaudron, 1988). Undoubtedly, recast is an economic way of correction, since it does not take up a lot of time. Besides, as an implicit negative feedback, recast does not draw as much attention as other feedback techniques. Thus it is less likely to be a potential source of embarrassment. For LP students, students with low self-esteem and students with high L2 confidence, teachers can employ this technique on some occasions. To call students' attention to teachers' corrective behavior, teachers can use paralinguistic means, such as pitch and intonation to accompany recast.

As mentioned before, positive affective feedback should be regarded as the prerequisite of error correction (Vigil and Oller, 1976). Whether teachers' corrective behavior is effective or not was largely determined by their attitude and wording in treating students' errors. Zhang and Dai (2001) suggested that corrections without threat to one's "face" were easier to be accepted. Praise and other ways to express one's appreciation of students' contributions are of prime importance to counteract the potential threat to one's esteem engendered by cognitive negative feedback. According to the teachers surveyed in this study, they paid much attention to building up the students' confidence and giving them encouragement in instruction. This would enable the students to be open to the information that teachers provided through correction, thus promoting language development.

114

In face-to-face interaction, non-verbal behavior was thought to be as important as words that were spoken (Pennycook, 1985; Bancroft, 1997). Empirical evidence showed that gestures and other non-verbal behavior could reinforce verbal expressions to benefit second language learners (Allen, 1995; Cabrera and Martinez, 2001; Lazaraton, 2004; Mori, 1998). For some high frequency errors, especially grammatical errors, teachers can make use of non-verbal means of feedback, for example, gestures. After the relationship between gestures and what they represent has been established, the students will find it easy to realize the existence of their errors and identify their nature. By this means time can be saved for correction. Besides, when the teachers use gesture to treat errors, the students are endowed with opportunities to make self-generated repairs. The threat brought by negative feedback can be avoided. It is the same with teachers' facial expressions. A puzzled expression, raised eye brows, a frown, a head shake, a hand shake, a sudden change of facial expression or posture can all be effective means to assist students to detect their errors. Proper use of non-verbal means can also activate the classroom atmosphere and make learning more interesting.

It was found that teachers tended to treat their students' errors after they finished with their expressions, which was in conformity with the NS's behavior in Day et al. 's (1984) study. It is an appropriate means taken in communication-focused activities (Dai and Niu, 1999). On-the-spot correction and correction upon the completion of a sentence are helpful in that teachers' feedback will leave a relatively deep impression on the students. What is detrimental is that such corrective behavior may break students' train of thought and frustrate them by calling their attention to the problems in their speech constantly. Comparatively, delayed correction is advantageous in that it does not interrupt students in the flow of communication. Nevertheless, after the students finish with their interaction in class, a feeling of relief may distract some

115

students' attention from what the teacher say about their performance. The failure of noticing the teacher's negative feedback makes it impossible for them to realize the existent problems they have. Corresponding actions will not be taken to make necessary reformulations and adjustments. Besides, when the teacher pinpoints the problems in students' speech upon their completion of the whole expression, students may get a little confused, for they may have forgotten when and how they have committed errors. It takes time to help the students recall what they have said. What's more, delayed correction can only be employed to point out most serious errors. A large number of errors requiring treatment may slip by. It seems that to decide on when to treat errors is a demanding task. What the teacher needs is a keen sense, flexibility and constant reflection. Different measures should be taken under different circumstances, with regard to the nature of errors, students' proficiency and personality and classroom atmosphere.

As Edge (1989) pointed out, peer correction in whole-class activities was advantageous in four aspects. Firstly, both the error producer and the corrector are involved in listening to and thinking about the language. Secondly, when encouraging students to correct their peers' errors, the teacher can obtain information of the learners' language ability. Thirdly, peer correction enables the learners to learn to cooperate so as to be less dependent on their teachers. Fourthly, after students get used to the idea of correcting each other without hurting others or being hurt, they will be able to help each other to improve in doing pair or group work. It is advisable that the teachers create more opportunities to enable students to correct other's errors in class, especially for high frequency errors. Apart from the advantages mentioned above, this means can also focus all students' attention on what is going on in class and help heighten their awareness of errors. Worthy of note is the classroom atmosphere and the way peer correction is made. The teacher should take caution not to let the error producers feel devalued or frustrated.

In doing pair/group work, students tended to recast their peers' errors most often. Since pair/group work in our classroom is mostly meaning-oriented rather than form-oriented, teachers can encourage students to negotiate for meaning. Feedback triggering interactional modifications will promote learning. Furthermore, such techniques as clarification request and questioning will generate self-repair, which can help with the proceduralization of internalized knowledge and increase students' sensitivity to errors. At the same time, students' communicative competence has been improved.

Chapter Five   Conclusion

5.1 Major findings

Major findings of this study can be summarized as follows:

1. Both EM teacher group and NEM teacher group did not over-react to students' errors. Teachers were not critical upon the occurrence of students' errors on the whole. The type of errors they treated most frequently was expression errors. Next were grammatical errors and pronunciation errors. The techniques employed most by teachers were recast and elicitation. Some teachers made use of non-verbal means in providing negative feedback. Most of the teachers corrected student errors after the students finished with their expressions. Teachers' corrective behavior differed when students were engaged in teacher-centered activities and pair/group work.

2. The difference between EM teacher group and NEM teacher group mainly consisted in: 1) EM teachers corrected their students less often than NEM teachers. 2) EM teachers treated expression errors more than NEM teachers, while NEM teachers treated grammatical and pronunciation errors more. 3) EM teachers used clarification request more than NEM teachers, while NEM teachers used explicit correction and metalinguistic feedback more.

3. A majority of teachers did take individual differences into account in providing negative feedback. They corrected LP students, female students, students with low self-esteem, low risk-takers and students with high level of language anxiety less often. They employed different means of correction to extroverts and introverts, HP students and LP students, students with high self-esteem and students with low self-esteem, high risk-takers and low risk-

takers and students with high level of language anxiety and students with low level of language anxiety.

4. The students held a positive attitude towards errors and error correction. However, they did not want error to be corrected too frequently. Two types of errors put at the top of their priority list, which were worth great attention in error treatment, were pronunciation errors and expression errors. The students preferred corrective techniques leading to self-repair. English majors had a stronger desire to be offered the opportunities to correct errors by themselves. Students wanted their teachers to correct their errors upon their completion of expression. They approved of their teachers' different way of treating errors in whole-class activities and pair/group work. On the whole, teachers' corrective behavior could meet the students' needs.

5. The preferred corrective techniques of HP students, students with high self-esteem, high risk-takers and students with high L2 confidence were those leading to self-repair. For LP students, low risk-takers, students with high language anxiety level and students with low L2 confidence, their favorite corrective technique was recast.

6. Students' attitude toward peer correction was positive. They did not treat peers' errors frequently. They corrected their peers' pronunciation errors most often and recast erroneous expressions most frequently in peer correction.

7. HP students, extroverts, students with high self-esteem, high risk-takers, students with low language anxiety level and students with high L2 confidence tended to provide their peers with more opportunities for self-repair. LP students and students with low self-esteem often used recast. Low risk-takers and students with low L2 confidence liked to correct their peers' errors explicitly.

8. In pair/group work HP students, extroverts and high risk-takers preferred corrective techniques leading to self-repair more than LP students, introverts and low risk-takers. Students with high language anxiety level were fond of recast, while students with low language anxiety level liked explicit correction best. Students with low L2 confidence preferred explicit correction, while students with high L2 confidence were in favor of recast.

5.2 Pedagogical implications

The present study has investigated the attitude of EM teachers and NEM teachers towards students' linguistic errors in classroom interaction and their corrective behavior. English majors' and non-English majors' needs and preferences concerned with negative feedback provision in whole-class activities and student-centered pair/group work have been explored. Besides, the differences among students with different proficiency, personality, language anxiety level and L2 confidence have been analyzed in detail. The findings provide language teachers with valuable information as to how to deal with students' linguistic errors properly in classroom interactions and how to assist the students to benefit most from classroom activities by giving and receiving feedback.

When deciding whether and how to treat errors, teachers should take several factors into account, namely, seriousness of the error, frequency of error occurrence, purpose of the activity, difficulty of the task, students' proficiency level and personality and reactions of the audience as well. To prevent fossilization of linguistic items, it is of great importance that teachers adjust the learners' faulty hypotheses in time. However, with regard to the limited time in class and students' psychological needs, it is impossible for the teacher to treat all the errors students made. Since the purpose of classroom activities is mainly to develop students' ability in using English for expression, the primary concern for the teacher should be communicative effect of the utterances. Only those global errors that may lead to misunderstanding or communication failure should be treated immediately. Besides, requirement of the curriculum is also an important factor to be considered. If the deviation in learner's utterance suggests incomplete knowledge he/she has about the language points or structures that have been pedagogical foci, effective measures should be taken to help the

120

student to assimilate the linguistic knowledge into their current language system. Another factor counting much is whether the errors are unacceptable and likely to arouse irritation of the native speakers in their culture. These errors are detrimental to the relationship and communication between the speakers and their native speaker counterparts. Moreover, such errors are often committed for lack of sufficient linguistic knowledge. Since the presence of these errors seldom influences the smooth flow of information, the chance for them to get treated is slim. Without timely treatment, these errors are very likely to fossilize.

On treating students' errors, the teacher should employ different corrective techniques be employed under different circumstances. Given the time allowed for error treatment, nature of the errors, students' personality, their language proficiency and ability to self-correct, the teacher can choose to make his/her corrective behavior explicit or implicit, to allow the learner opportunity for self-repair or provide the correct version directly. No matter what kind of negative feedback is given, it should be accompanied by positive affective feedback. Anxiety that learners experience in foreign language classrooms is stronger than in other classrooms. It was found that the concern about negative evaluation from the teacher and peers was the major source of language anxiety. Because the teacher is a valued person whose opinion and behavior may have considerable influence on the students' self-evaluations, his/her positive feedback is of paramount importance to help students persist in their study and stimulate them to advance further. No wonder all the students who were interviewed stated that they found praise from their teachers encouraging and motivating.

As findings of this study revealed, students, whether good or poor in English, wanted to modify their erroneous expressions by themselves when they were able to self-repair. For some students, especially English majors and HP students, the sense of responsibility urges them

121

to make necessary adjustments, for they know timely correction is of vital importance to benefit them in their future study. To some students self-repair leaves deeper impression on them than other means of correction. For others, especially some poor students and those students with low self-esteem or low L2 confidence, self-correction is a way to declare one's capability to do things well, which brings about a sense of achievement and helps regain one's "face". Therefore, it is advisable that teachers should use techniques generating self-repair as much as possible. With a mere nudge or hints from the teacher, learning in the part of the learners may be greatly enhanced. Many researchers have called for teachers to increase wait-time in class to enable students to answer teachers' questions with higher quality. In treating students' errors we can also give our students more time and opportunities to reformulate their ill-formed or inappropriate expressions.

Though allowing students to self-repair is beneficial, it does not mean that the techniques triggering self-generated repair can be employed at any time. When the errors are made because of the students' incomplete target language resources, self-correction on the part of the students themselves seems infeasible. At this time the provision of correct versions and explanations may be more desirable. Besides, for some students who are highly anxious, pushing them to make reformulations will increase their anxiety level and embarrass them. Since these learners do not have adequate processing ability to find the proper way to modify their expressions, a sense of frustration arises. In this sense corrective techniques generating self-repair will be deleterious to these students' study rather than enhance their learning.

It was revealed that most teachers realized the significance of taking individual differences of students into account in negative feedback provision. The employment of effective feedback techniques fine-tuned to the need of individual students entails familiarity with them and knowledge about their proficiency, personality and preferences. From

122

the interviews it could be detected that our college teachers did not have much time to get along with students and some did not care much about individual students' needs and wants. Different techniques are suitable for different students on different occasions. Flexibility and adaptability in instruction is of great importance. To employ different means of correction in whole-class activities and pair/group work was understandable. It seemed that students were more open to various kinds of corrections in pair/group work. Teachers could change their way of error treatment constantly to meet students' needs.

With the advocacy of task-based language learning, classroom activities come to play a significant role in helping learners improve language skills. Students are provided with ample opportunities to produce the target language and get input and feedback from their partners in turn. As student-student interactions are important means for learners to gain exposure to the target language, it is better to ensure that the language that the students use is as target-like as possible. We language teachers can encourage students to provide their partners with negative feedback, ask for clarification, or, at least, state their doubts openly whenever communicative problems arise. Discussion on the usage of linguistic items and structures stimulates the students to think, activates their linguistic resources and enables them to broaden their horizon and promote development. If the problems cannot be solved through discussion or reference to the dictionary, the teacher can offer timely assistance. The corrections provided at the time when students feel the need to restructure or expand their language knowledge system will be most beneficial. For peer correction to be effective, what counts is the attitude of the correctors. As long as the corrector can make his/her partner realize that he/she is to offer help instead of state criticism, the corrective behavior will be found acceptable and desirable.

What we can do in class to facilitate students' learning is limited. The errors receiving treatment only account for a small proportion. Since a large number of errors are left uncorrected, great attention should be paid to the increase of students' sensitivity to errors, especially those errors resulting from fatigue, anxiety or slips of tongue, which can be self-corrected. When the students are aware of the presence of these errors, they can avoid making the errors again. Frequency of these errors' occurrence will be lower after sufficient practice, with already internalized knowledge automatized. To enhance the students' awareness of errors, the teacher can encourage them to recall what errors they have made after they finish with their speech. Some errors within the students' reach can be self-corrected or receive peer correction. Others indicating students' lack of knowledge may get timely treatment of the teacher. When the good habit of reflection has been developed, students will benefit considerably for their further study. Besides, students can be asked to watch video or listen to some tapes to comment on the language used by the actors or speakers. They can also be asked to make tape-recordings of their own conversations and edit them by correcting errors. With high awareness of errors, the students can progress more rapidly.

5.3 Limitations of the study

First, the subjects of the present study include three hundred and fifty-two college students and eighty teachers. Though the sample is large enough for eliciting revealing findings, with regard to the large population receiving and giving classroom instruction in China and differences existing in colleges and universities, choosing more subjects can make the picture clearer. Especially for English-majors, since female students accounted for an overwhelming majority, the difference between male students and female students in their needs and preferences could not be explored deeply for the present study. If there was a larger sample, the distinction resulting from students' individual differences could be shown more explicitly.

Secondly, to ensure that results of the research can be generalized, I have studied students from several universities. Some are key universities under the direct administration of the Ministry of Education, some not. It is possible that the teaching methods employed by teachers, the way they organize their classroom activities, their expectations and requests of their students and their reactions to learners' insufficient L2 knowledge may vary. The students' needs and preferences may also differ when their proficiency level, their educational background and the learning environments were taken into account. When statistical calculations were made with all the subjects included in present study, the general tendency of error treatment in EFL classrooms could be detected. To get a comprehensive picture, further research should be carried out to investigate the teachers' teaching behavior and students' preferences in different learning contexts.

Thirdly, the findings of the present study were mostly based on self-reported data. Though I have endeavored to ensure that distortion would be made as little as possible in the process of data collection, nobody can guarantee that self-reported data is one hundred percent reliable. Probability exists that subjects give false information to beautify themselves or to please their teacher or the researcher. The result of the classroom observation I made in a previous study and the interviews subsequently made proved that the data collected were generally successful in eliciting the truth. The more convincing way of analysis and exploration was to be present in classes and observe how teachers and students behave in class.

Fourthly, interactional patterns and the way errors receive negative feedback may vary with the tasks students are engaged in. Free conversations and problem-solving tasks may trigger different corrective behavior of teachers and students. Classroom interactions with much focus on form after the learning of a new TL structure may differ considerably from conversations aiming at exchange of information. So are the corrections. Because of the limited time, I did not make distinctions as to what specific activities students were involved in. Further studies should be conducted to get answers to this.

References

Allwright, R. 1975. Problems in the study of the language teacher's treatment of learner error. In M. Burt and H. Dulay (Eds.), *New Directions in Second Language Learning, Teaching and Bilingual Education.* Selected papers from the Ninth Annual TESOL Convention: Los Angeles, March 1975. Washington, D. C.: TESOL.

Allwright, D. & Bailey, K. 1991. *Focus on the language classroom: an introduction classroom research for language teachers.* Cambridge: Cambridge University Press.

Ayoun, D. 2001. The role of negative and positive feedback in the second language acquisition of the passé compose and imparfait. *Modern Language Journal*, 85, 226–243.

Basturkmen, H., Loewen, S. & Ellis, R. 2004. Teachers' stated beliefs about incidental focus on form and their classroom practices. *Applied Linguistics*, 25, 243–272.

Becker, J. 1975. The phrasal lexicon. In B. Nash-Webber and R. Schank (Eds), *Theoretical Issues in Natural Language Processing Vol. 1* Bolt, Baranek and Newman, Cambridge, MA. pp. 70–73.

Benson, C. 2002. Transfer/cross-linguistic influence. *ELT Journal*, 56, 68–70.

Beretta, A. 1989. Attention to form or meaning? Error treatment in the Bangalore project. *TESOL Quarterly*, 23, 283–303.

Birdstrong, D. 1989. *Metalinguistic performance and interlinguitic competence.* Berlin: Springer-Verlag.

Braidi, S. 2002. Reexamining the role of recasts in native-speaker/ nonnative-speaker interactions. *Language Learning*, 52, 1 – 42.

Brumfit, C. 1983. Communicative language teaching: an educational perspective. In C. Brumfit and K. Johnson (Eds.), *The communicative approach to language teaching*. Oxford: Oxford University Press.

Bruton, A. & Samuda, V. 1980. Learner and teacher roles in the treatment of oral error in group work. *RELC Journal*, 11, 49 – 63.

Burt, M. 1975. Error analysis in the adult EFL classroom. *TESOL Quarterly*, 9, 53 – 63.

Cabrera, M. & Martinez, P. 2001. The effects of repetition, comprehension checks and gestures on primary school children in an EFL situation. *ELT Journal*, 55, 281 – 288.

Carroll, S. & Swain, M. 1993. Explicit and implicit negative feedback: An empirical study of the learning of linguistic generalizations. *Studies in Second Language Acquisition*, 15, 357 – 386.

Carroll, S. ,Roberge, Y. & Swain, M. 1992. The role of feedback in adult second language acquisition: error correction and morphological generalizations. *Applied Psycholinguistics*, 13, 173 – 198.

Cathcart, R. and Olsen, J. 1976. Teachers' and students' preferences for correction of classroom conversation errors. In J. Fanselow & R. Crymes (Eds.), *On TESOL 76* (pp. 41 – 53). Washington, D. C. TESOL.

Chaudron, C. 1977. A descriptive model of discourse in the corrective treatment of learners' errors. *Language Learning*, 27, 29 – 46.

Chaudron, C. 1986. Teachers' priorities in correcting learners' errors in French immersion classes. In R. Day (Ed.), *Talking to learn: Conversation in second language acquisition* (pp. 64 – 84). Rowley, MA: Newbury House.

Chaudron, C. 1988. *Second language classrooms*. New York: Cambridge

University Press.

Chenoweth, N. , Day, R. , Chun, A. &Luppescu, S. 1983. Attitudes and preferences of ESL students to error correction. *Studies in Second Language Acquisition*, 6, 79 – 87.

Chomsky, N. 1965. *Aspects of the theory of syntax.* Cambridge, Mass: MIT Press.

Chun, A. , Day, R. , Chenweth, N. & Luppescu, S. 1982. Errors, interaction and correction: A study of native-nonnative conversations. *TESOL Quarterly*, 16, 537 – 547.

Corder, S. 1967. The significance of learners' errors. *IRAL*, 5, 161 – 170.

Corder, S. 1977. *Introducing applied linguistics.* Harmondsworth, Middlesex: Penguin Books Ltd.

Corder, S. 1981. *Error analysis and interlanguage.* Oxford University Press.

Courchene, R. 1980. The error analysis hypothesis, the contrastive analysis hypothesis, and the correction of error in the second language classroom. *TESL Talk*, 11/2, 3 – 13 and 11/3, 10 – 29.

Crookes, G. and Rulon, K. 1988. Topic continuation and corrective feedback in native-nonnative conversation. *TESOL Quarterly*, 22, 675 – 681.

Davies, E. 1983. Error evaluation: the importance of viewpoint. *English Language Teaching Journal*, 37, 304 – 311.

Day, R. , Chenoweth, N. , Chun, A. &Luppescu, S. 1984. Corrective feedback in native-nonnative discourse. *Language Learning*, 34, 19 – 45.

de Bot, K. 1996. The psycholinguistics of the output hypothesis. *Language Learning*, 46, 529 – 555.

Donato, R. 1994. Collective scaffolding in second language learning. In J. Lantolf & G. . Appel, (Eds.), *Vygotskian approaches to second*

129

language research (pp. 33 - 56). Norwood, NJ: Ablex.

Doughty, C. 1994. Fine-tuning of feedback by competent speakers to language learners. In J. Alatis (Ed.), *GURT 1993* (pp. 96 - 108). Washington, DC: Georgetown University Press.

Doughty, C. & Varela, E. 1998. Communicative focus on form. In C. Doughty & J. Williams (Eds.), *Focus on form in classroom SLA* (pp. 114 - 138). New York: Cambridge University Press.

Dulay, H. and Burt, M. 1974. Errors and strategies in child second language acquisition. *TESOL Quarterly*, 8, 129 - 36.

Dulay, H., Burt, M., & Krashen, S. 1982. *Language two*. New York: Oxford University Press.

Eckman, F. 1977. Markedness and the contrastive analysis hypothesis. *Language Learning*, 27, 315 - 20.

Edge, J. 1989. *Mistakes and correction*. Harlow: Longman.

Ellis, N. 1995. Consciousness in second language acquisition: a review of field studies and laboratory experiments. *Language Awareness*, 4, 123 - 146.

Ellis, R. 1984. Can syntax be taught? A study of the effects of formal instruction on the acquisition of WH questions by children. *Applied Linguistics*, 5, 138 - 155.

Ellis, R., Basturkmen, H., & Loewen, S. 2001. Learner uptake in communicative ESL lessons. *Language Learning*, 51, 281 - 318

Fanselow, J. 1977. The treatment of error in oral work. *Foreign Language Annals*, 10, 583 - 593.

Farrar, M. 1990. Discourse and the acquisition of grammatical morphemes. *Journal of Child Language*, 17, 607 - 624.

Farrar, M. 1992. Negative evidence and grammatical morpheme acquisition. *Developmental Psychology*, 28, 90 - 98.

Foss, K. and Reitzel, A. 1988. A relational model for managing second language anxiety. *TESOL Quarterly*, 22, 437 - 54.

Gaskill, W. 1980. Correction in native-nonnative speaker conversation. In D. Larsen-Freeman (Ed.), *Discourse analysis in second language research* (pp. 125 – 137). Rowley, MA: Newbury House.

Gass, S. 1984. A review of interlanguage syntax: Language transfer and language universals. *Language Learning*, 34, 115 – 132.

Gass, S. & Selinker, L. 1994. *Second language acquisition: an introductory course*. Hillsdale, NJ: Erlbaum.

Gass, S. & Varonis, E. 1994. Input, interaction, and second language production. *Studies in Second Language Acquisition*, 16, 283 – 302.

Ghadessy, M. 1985. The role of developmental errors in assessing language competence. ELT Journal, 39, 262 – 266.

Granger, S. 1996. Romance words in English: from history to pedagogy. In J. Svartvik (Ed.), *Words: KVHAA Conference 36* (pp. 105 – 21). Almquist & Wiksell, Stockholm. .

Grauberg, W. 1971. An error analysis in German of first-year university student. In G. Perren and J. Trim (Eds.), *Applications of Linguistics* (pp. 257 – 263), Cambridge University Press, Cambridge.

Haded, M. 1998. The merits of exploiting error analysis in foreign language teaching and learning. *RELC*, 55 – 65.

Hammerly, H. 1987. The immersion approach: Litmus test of second language acquisition through classroom communication. *Modern Language Journal*, 71, 395 – 401.

Han, Z. 2002. A study of the impact of recasts on tense consistency in L2 output. *TESOL Quarterly*, 36, 543 – 572.

Hendrickson, J. 1978. Error correction in foreign language teaching: Recent theory, research, and practice. *Modern Language Journal*, 62, 387 – 398.

Herron, C. & Tomasello, M. 1988. Learning grammatical structures in a foreign language: modeling versus feedback. *The French Review*, 61, 910 – 923.

Higgs, T. and Clifford, R. 1982. The push toward communication. In T. Higgs (Ed.), *Curriculum, competence and the foreign language teacher* (pp. 57 – 79). Skokie, IL: National Textbook.

Horwitz, E. & Young, D. 1991. *Language learning anxiety: from theory and research to classroom implications.* Englewood Cliffs, NJ: Prentice Hall.

Hughes, A & Lascaratou, C. 1982. Competing criteria for error gravity. *English Language Teaching Journal*, 36: 175 – 182.

Ishida, M. 2004. Effects of recasts on the acquisition of aspectual form – te i- *(ru)* by learners of Japanese as a foreign language. *Language Learning*, 54, 311 – 394.

Izumi, S. 1998. *Negative feedback in adult NS-NNS task-based conversation.* Paper presented at the Annual Convention of the American Association of Applied Linguistics, Seattle, WA.

Izumi, S. 2000. Does output promote noticing and second language acquisition? *TESOL Quarterly*, 34, 230 – 278.

Jackson, H. 1987. The value of error analysis and its implications for teaching and therapy—with special reference to Panjabi learners. In J. Abudarhan (Ed.), *Bilingualism and the Bilingual: An Interdisciplinary Approach to Pedagogical and Remedial Issues* (pp. 100 – 111). Nelson for the National Foundation for Educational Research, Windsor and Philadelphia. .

James, C. 1998. *Errors in language learning and use: Exploring error analysis.* London: Longman.

James, C. and Persidou, M. 1993. Learners and acquirers: compensatory strategy preferences. In J. Fernandez-Barrientos Martin (Ed.), *Proceedings of the International Conference on Applied Linguistics Vol. 1* (pp. 344 – 59). University of Granada, Granada. .

Kaufmann, L. 1993. *Please correct me if I'm wrong.* Unpublished paper presented at the 10th AILA Congress, Amsterdam, August 1993.

Keys, K. 2002. First language influence on the spoken English of Brazilian students of EFL. *ELT Journal*, 56, 43 - 46.

Khalil, A. 1985. Communicative error evaluation: Native speaker's evaluation and interpretation of written errors of Arab EFL learners. *TESOL Quarterly*, 19, 335 - 351.

Laufer, B. 1992. Native language effect on confusion of similar lexical forms. In C. Mair and M. Markus (Eds), *New Departures in Contrastive Linguistics: Innsbrucker Beiträge zur Kulturwissenschaft Vol. 2* (pp. 199 - 209). University of Innsbruck, Innsbruck.

Lazaraton, A. 2004. Gesture and speech in the vocabulary explanations of one ESL teacher: a microanalytic Inquiry. *Language Learning*, 54, 79 - 117.

Lennon, P. 1991. Error: Some problems of definition, identification, and distinction. *Applied Linguistics*, 12, 181 - 196.

Lightbown, P. & Spada, N. 1990. Focus-on-form and corrective feedback in communicative language teaching: Effects on second language learning. *Studies in Second Language Acquisition*, 12, 429 - 448.

Lin, Y. & Hedgcock, J. 1996. Negative feedback incorporation among high-proficiency and low-proficiency Chinese-speaking learners of Spanish. *Language Learning*, 46, 567 - 611.

Liski, E. & Puntanen, S. 1983. A study of the statistical foundations of group conversation tests in spoken English. *Language Learning*, 23.

Loewen, S. 2004. Uptake in incidental focus on form in meaning-focused ESL lessons. *Language Learning*, 54, 153 - 188.

Long, M. 1988. Instructed interlanguage development. In L. Beebe (Ed.), *Issues in second language acquisition: Multiple perspectives* (pp. 115 - 141). Cambridge, MA: Newbury House.

Long, M. 1996. The role of the linguistic environment in second language acquisition. In W. Ritchie & T. Bhatia (Eds.), *Handbook of language acquisition. Vol. 2: Second Language Acquisition* (pp. 413 – 468). New York: Academic.

Long, M. , Inagaki, S. & Ortega, L. 1998. The role of implicit negative feedback in SLA: Models and recasts in Japanese and Spanish. *Modern Language Journal*, 82, 357 – 371.

Lyster, R. 1998a. Negotiation of form, recasts, and explicit correction in relation to error types and learner repair in immersion classrooms. *Language Learning*, 48, 183 – 218.

Lyster, R. 1998b. Recasts, repetition, and ambiguity in L2 classroom discourse. *Studies in Second Language Acquisition*, 20, 51 – 81.

Lyster, R. & Ranta, L. 1997. Corrective feedback and learner uptake: Negotiation of form in communicative classrooms. *Studies in Second Language Acquisition*, 19, 37 – 66.

MacIntyre, P & Gardner, R. 1991. Investigating language class anxiety using the focused essay technique. *Modern Language Journal*, 75, 296 – 304.

Mackey, A. 1995. *Stepping up the pace: Input interaction and interlanguage development. An empirical study of questions in ESL.* Unpublished doctoral dissertation, University of Sydney, Sydney, Australia.

Mackey, A. 2000. *Feedback, noticing and second language development: An empirical study of L2 classroom interaction.* Paper presented at the British Association for Applied Linguistics Conference 2000, Cambridge, U. K.

Mackey, A. 2003. International input and the incorporation of feedback: an exploration of NS-NNS and NNS-NNS adult and child dyads. *Language Learning*, 53, 35 – 66.

Mackey, A. and J. Philp. 1998. Conversational interaction and second language development: Recasts, responses, and red herrings? *Modern Language Journal*, 82, 338 – 356.

McCargar, D. 1993. Teacher and student role expectations: Cross-cultural differences and implications. *Modern Language Journal*, 77, 192 - 207.

McCroskey, J. 1977. Oral communication apprehension: A summary of recent theory and research. *Human Communication Research*, 4, 78 - 96.

Meara, P. 1984. The study of lexis in interlanguage. In A. Davies, C. Criper and Howatt. (Eds), *Interlanguage: Papers in Honor of S. Pit Corder* (pp. 225 - 235). Edinburgh University Press, Edinburgh.

Mito, K. 1993. *The effects of modeling and recasting on the acquisition of L2 grammar rules*. Unpublished manuscript, University of Hawaii, Manoa.

Morris, F. and Tarone, E. 2003. Impact of classroom dynamics on the effectiveness of recasts in second language acquisition. *Language Learning* 53, 325 - 368.

Muranoi, H. 2000. Focus on form through interaction enhancement: Intergrating formal instruction with a communicative task in EFL classrooms. *Language Learning*, 50, 617 - 673

Murphy, D. 1986. Communication and correction in the classroom. *ELT Journal*, 40, 146 - 151.

Nattinger, J. & Carrica, J. 1992. *Lexical phrases and language teaching*. Oxford University Press, Oxford.

Nelson, K. 1987. Some observations from the perspective of the rare event cognitive comparison theory of language acquisition. In K. Nelson and A. vanKleeck (Eds.), *Children's Language Vol. 6* (pp. 411 - 445). Hillsdale, NJ: Erbaum.

Nelson, K. 1991. On differentiated language-learning models and differentiated interventions. In N. Krasnegor, D. Rumbaugh, R. Schiefelbusch & M. Studdert-Kennedy (Eds.), *Biological and Behavioral Determinants of language development* (pp. 399 - 428).

Hillsdale, NJ: Erlbaum.

Nobuyoshi, J. , & Ellis, R. 1993. Focused communication tasks and second language acquisition. *ELT Journal*, 47, 203 – 210.

Norrish, J. 1983. *Language learners and their errors*. Macmillan Publishers.

Nystrom, N. 1983. Teacher-student interaction in bilingual classrooms: four approaches to error feedback. In H. Seliger & M. Long (Eds.), *Classroom oriented research in second language acquisition* (pp. 169 – 189). Rowley, Mass: Newbury House.

Oliver, R. 1995. Negative feedback in child NS-NNS conversation. *Studies in Second Language Acquisition*, 17, 459 – 481.

Oliver, R. 2000. Age differences in negotiation and feedback in classroom and pair work. *Language Learning*, 50, 119 – 151.

Oliver, R. & Mackey, A. 2003. International context and feedback in child ESL classrooms. *Modern Language Journal*, 87, 519 – 533.

Ortega, L. , & Long, M. 1997. The effects of models and recasts on the acquisition of object topicalization and adverb placement in L2 Spanish. *Spanish Applied Linguistics*, 1, 65 – 86.

Pasty, L. , & S. Nina. 1993. *How languages are learned*. Oxford University Press.

Pawley, A. & Syder, F.. 1983. Two puzzles for linguistic theory: nativelike selection and nativelike fluency. In J. Richards and R. Schmidt (Eds), *Language and Communication* (pp. 191 – 226), Longman, London.

Penner, S. 1987. Parental responses to grammatical and ungrammatical child utterance. *Child Development*, 58, 376 – 384.

Philp, J. 2003. Constraints on "noticing the gap": Nonnative speakers' noticing of recasts in NS-NNS interaction. *Studies in Second Language Acquisition*, 25, 99 – 126.

Pica, T. , Porter, F. , Paninos, D. & Linnell J. 1996. Language learners' interaction: how does it address the input, output, and feedback needs of L2 learners? *TESOL Quarterly*, 30, 59 - 84.

Pienemann, M. 1985. Learnability and syllabus construction. In K. Hyltenstam & M. Pienemann (Eds.), *Modeling and assessing second language acquisition* (pp. 23 - 75). Clevedon, England: Multilingual Matters.

Pienemann, M. 1989. Is language teachable? Psycholinguistic experiments and hypothesis. *Applied Linguistics*, 10, 52 - 79.

Pienemann, M. 1999. *Language processing and second language development: processibility theory*. Amsterdam: John Benjamins.

Phillips, E. 1992. The effects of language anxiety on students' oral test performance and attitudes. *Modern Language Journal*, 76, 14 - 26.

Richard, R. and Rod, B. 1990. *Currents of change in English language teaching*. Oxford University Press.

Richards, J. 1971. Error analysis and second language strategies. *Language Sciences*, 17, 12 - 22.

Richards, J. 1998. *The context of language teaching*. Cambridge University Press.

Richards, J. , Platt, J. & Platt, H. 1992. *Longman dictionary of language teaching and applied linguistics*. Longman.

Richardson, M. 1993. *Negative evidence and grammatical morpheme acquisition: implications for SLA*. Unpublished manuscript, University of Western Australia, Nedlands.

Santos, T. 1987. Markedness theory and error evaluation: an experimental study. *Applied Linguistics*, 8, 207 - 218.

Schachter J. 1981. The hand signal system. *TOSEL Quarterly*, 15, 125 - 138.

Schachter, J. 1984. A universal input condition. In W. Rutherford (Ed.), *Universals and second language acquisition*. Amsterdam, Netherlands: John Banjamins.

137

Schmidt, R. 1990. The role of consciousness in second language learning. *Applied Linguistics*, 11, 206 - 226.

Schmidt, R. 1993. Awareness and second language acquisition. *Annual Review of Applied Linguistics*, 13, 206 - 226.

Schmidt, R. 1994. Deconstructing consciousness in search of useful definitions for applied linguistics. *AILA Review*, 11, 11 - 26

Schmidt, R. & Frota, S. 1986. Developing basic conversational ability in a second language: A case study of an adult learner of Portuguese. In R. Day (Ed.), *Talking to learn* (pp. 237 - 326). Rowley, MA: Newbury House.

Schulz, R. 2001. Cultural differences in student and teacher perceptions concerning the role of grammar instruction and corrective feedback: USA-Colombia. *Modern Language Journal*, 85, 244 - 258.

Selinker, L. 1992. *Rediscovering interlanguage*. London: Longman.

Sheorey, R. 1986. Error perceptions of native-speaking and non-native speaking teachers of ESL. *English Language Teaching Journal*, 40, 306 - 312.

Spada, N. , & Lightbown, P. 1993. Instruction and the development of questions in L2 classrooms. *Studies in Second Language Acquisition*, 15, 205 - 224.

Swain, M. 1985. Communicative competence: Some roles of comprehensible input and comprehensible output in its development. In S. Gass & C. Madden (Eds.), *Input in second language acquisition* (pp. 235 - 253). Rowley, MA: Newbury House.

Swain, M. 1995. Three functions of output in second language learning. In G. Cook & B. Seidhofer(Eds.), *Principle and practice in applied linguistics: Studies in honour of H. G. Widdowson* (pp. 125 - 144). Oxford: Oxford University Press.

Swain, M. & Carroll, S. 1987. The immersion observation study. In B. Harley, P. Allen, J. Cummins, & M. Swain (Eds.), *The* development of bilingual proficiency final report : *Classroom treatment Vol. 2* (pp. 190 – 342). Toronto : Modern Language Center, The Ontario Institute for Studies in Education.

Thornbury, S. 1999. *How to teach grammar*. Essex : Pearson Education Limited.

Tobias, S. 1979. Anxiety research in educational psychology. *Journal of Educational Psychology*, 71 , 573 – 582.

Tobias, S. 1986. Anxiety and cognitive processing of instruction. In R. Schwarzer (Ed.) , *Self-related cognition in anxiety and motivation*. Hillsdale, New Jersey : Lawrence Erlbaum Associates.

Tomasello, M. and Herron, C. 1989. Feedback for language transfer errors : the garden path technique. *Studies in Second Language Acquisition*, 11 , 385 – 395.

Tomiyama, M. 1980. Grammatical errors communication breakdown. *TESOL Quarterly*, 14.

White, H. 1977. *Error analysis and error correction in adult learners of English as a second language*. Working Papers on Bilingualism 13 : 42 – 58.

White, L. 1990. Implications of learnability theories for second language learning and teaching. In M. Halliday, J. Gibbons, & H. Nicholas (Eds.) , *Learning keeping and using language. Amsterdam* : John Benjamins.

White, L. 1991. Adverb placement in second language acquisition : Some effects of positive and negative evidence in the classroom. *Second Language Research*, 7 , 133 – 161.

Williams, J. 2001. The effectiveness of spontaneous attention to from. *System*, 29 , 325 – 340.

van Lier, L. 1988. *The classroom and the language learner*. London : Longman

Vigil, N. , & Oller, J. 1976. Rule fossilization : A tentative model.

Language Learning, 26, 281 – 295.

戴炜栋、牛强. 1999. 过渡语的石化现象及其教学启示. 外语研究, 第 2 期, 10 – 15.

文秋芳. 1996. 英语学习策略论. 上海外语教育出版社.

文秋芳. 2001. 从全国英语专业四级口试看口语教学. 外语界, 第 4 期, 24 – 28.

张雪梅、戴炜栋. 2001. 反馈　二语习得　语言教学. 外语界, 第 2 期, 2 – 8.

朱明慧. 1996. 英语口语课中的纠错策略. 外语界, 第 3 期, 32 – 34.

Appendixes

Appendix Ⅰ Questionnaire for teachers

问 卷 调 查

学校_____所教班级_____

姓名_____性别_____年龄_____

本问卷旨在了解老师对待**学生课堂发言**中所犯错误的态度以及纠错情况,希望您认真耐心地填写,所获得的数据对该问题的研究十分重要。

非 常 感 谢 您 的 配 合 !

一、请在下列各题中选出适当选项,**将答案写在横线上**。除了有特别说明的题目外,其余均为单选题。有些题目需加以说明,请在空格处填上您的想法。

1. 对于语言错误,我同意_____。

1)错误是失败的代名词,应尽量避免。

2)错误是语言学习过程中的重要组成部分,有积极作用。

2. 在课堂发言中,您的学生_____意识到自己的语言错误。

1)总是能   2)经常能

3)有时能   4)极少能

5)从不能

3. 您在学生上课发言时更注重其_____。

1)语言形式   2)表达内容

4. 您在上课时_____纠正学生的语言错误。

    1）总是   2）经常

    3）有时   4）极少

    5）从不

5. 学生在口语表达中常出现这样几类错误:语音错误、语法错误、词汇错误、表达错误(即看似正确,却不符合英语表达习惯的错误)和语篇错误(即符合语法和表达习惯,但从上文看让人无法理解的错误)。您的学生在课堂发言中最常出现的是_____(可选一到两项)。

    1）语音错误   2）语法错误

    3）词汇错误   4）表达错误

    5）语篇错误

6. 在学生课堂发言所出现的各类错误中,您通常纠正最多的是_____(可选一到两项),原因是_____。

    1）语音错误   2）语法错误

    3）词汇错误   4）表达错误

    5）语篇错误

7. 您认为哪类错误应首先得到纠正,哪类错误次之? 请在括号中填入 1—5,最有必要纠正的错误填 1,次之的填 2,依此类推。

    语音错误（   ）   语法错误（   ）

    词汇错误（   ）   表达错误（   ）

    语篇错误（   ）

8. 课堂上您在决定是否纠正学生的语言错误时,通常会考虑以下各因素。您首先考虑的因素是_____(请填一到两项)。请按重要程度给以下各项排序,最重要的因素填1,次之填2,依此类推,填入 1—7(8)。

    1）错误是否会引起本国语者的反感(   )

    2）错误是否与刚学的语言点或本课重点有关(   )

3）错误是否在学生的发言中屡次出现（　　　）

4）错误是否为常用语,不纠正会使其他同学形成错误的概念（　　　）

5）错误是否影响了交流,会引起误解或不理解（　　　）

6）学生是否能自己意识到错误并能自己纠正（　　　）

7）学生的个体差异（　　　）

8）其他（请说明）＿＿＿＿＿＿＿＿＿＿＿＿＿＿＿＿＿＿。

就学生的个体差异,请您将下列五项按重要程度排序:

1）学生的性格（　　　）

2）学生的英语水平（　　　）

3）学生的自信心（　　　）

4）学生对英语水平的自信心（　　　）

5）学生使用英语时的焦虑程度（　　　）

9. 当您注意到学生发言中的错误并认为有必要纠正时,以下三种情况出现的频率如何?

　　——您在课上纠正:＿＿＿＿＿＿＿

1）总是　　　　　　　　　2）经常

3）有时　　　　　　　　　4）极少

5）从不

通常在下列情况下您在课上纠正错误:＿＿＿＿＿＿＿＿＿＿＿

＿＿＿＿＿＿＿＿＿＿＿＿＿＿＿＿＿＿＿＿＿＿＿＿＿＿＿＿＿

＿＿＿＿＿＿＿＿＿＿＿＿＿＿＿＿＿＿＿＿＿＿＿＿＿＿＿＿。

　　——您记下错误,以后和学生单独交流:＿＿＿＿＿＿＿

1）总是　　　　　　　　　2）经常

3）有时　　　　　　　　　4）极少

5）从不

通常在下列情况下您课后和学生单独交流:＿＿＿＿＿＿＿＿＿

＿＿＿＿＿＿＿＿＿＿＿＿＿＿＿＿＿＿＿＿＿＿＿＿＿＿＿＿＿

＿＿＿＿＿＿＿＿＿＿＿＿＿＿＿＿＿＿＿＿＿＿＿＿＿＿＿＿。

——您记下错误,以后集中讲解和练习:_____

1)总是　　　　　　　　2)经常
3)有时　　　　　　　　4)极少
5)从不

通常在下列情况下您在以后集中讲解和练习:_____
_____
_____。

10. 当学生的发言中出现错误,您通常何时纠错?_____
主要原因是_____
_____
_____。

1)立即纠正　　　　　　2)一句话说完后纠正
3)表达结束时纠正　　　4)上课时不纠正,课后纠正
5)以后纠正

11. 课堂纠错时,您采用以下方式纠错的频率怎样?
——明确纠正:明确指出错误所在并直接告知正确的表达
方式_____

1)总是　　　　　　　　2)经常
3)有时　　　　　　　　4)极少
5)从不

——重述:错误部分用正确形式替换_____

1)总是　　　　　　　　2)经常
3)有时　　　　　　　　4)极少
5)从不

——疑问:用升调重复错误部分_____

1)总是　　　　　　　　2)经常
3)有时　　　　　　　　4)极少
5)从不

——启发:通过具体问题或省略启发学生使用正确的表达
方式_____

1)总是　　　　　　　　2)经常

3）有时　　　　　　　　4）极少

5）从不

——要求说明:通过问题让学生重新表达 _____

1）总是　　　　　　　　2）经常

3）有时　　　　　　　　4）极少

5）从不

——元语言反馈:指出错误所属类别,提醒学生,让学生自己纠正_____

1）总是　　　　　　　　2）经常

3）有时　　　　　　　　4）极少

5）从不

——其他(请说明)_____

_____。

1）总是　　　　　　　　2）经常

3）有时　　　　　　　　4）极少

5）从不

12. 对于学生课堂发言中出现各类错误您是否采用不同方式纠错? _____。

1）是　　　　　　　　　2）不是

如果您选1,请在各类错误后的横线上填入纠错方式(可多选;如有其他方式,请直接写出)

语音错误_____　语法错误_____　词汇错误_____

表达错误_____　语篇错误_____

1）明确纠正　2）重述3）疑问　4）启发　5）要求说明

6）元语言反馈

13. 您认为最有效的纠错方式是_____,原因是_____

_____。

1）明确纠正　　　　　　2）重述

3）疑问　　　　　　　　4）启发

5）要求说明　　　　　　6）元语言反馈

7）其他:_____。

14. 您通常在这样的情况下让学生自己纠正错误_____

_____。

下面各组学生中,您通常让哪些学生自己纠错?请选择。
1) 外向学生　　　　　　　2) 内向学生
3) 性格外向和内向的学生都会_____
1) 男生　　　　　　　　　2) 女生
3) 男生和女生都会_____
1) 英语水平高的学生　　　2) 英语水平低的学生
3) 各种水平的学生都会_____
1) 很有自信的学生　　　　2) 缺乏自信的学生
3) 有没有自信的学生都会_____
1) 冒险性强的学生　　　　2) 冒险性弱的学生
3) 冒险性强和冒险性弱的学生都会_____
1) 发言时很紧张的学生　　2) 发言时不紧张的学生
3) 发言时很紧张和不紧张的学生都会_____

15. 在全班性课堂活动中您_____让其他同学纠正某位同学
的错误,原因是_____

_____。

1) 总是　　　　　　　　　2) 经常
3) 有时　　　　　　　　　4) 极少
5) 从不

16. 在全班性课堂活动和两人活动、小组讨论时,您在决定是否
纠错、如何纠错方面是否有所不同?_____
1) 是　　　　　　　　　　2) 否
如果您的选择是1,在决定是否纠错方面,不同之处表现在:

_____

_____。

在决定如何纠错方面,不同之处表现在:_____

_____

_____。

17. "学生互相纠错对英语学习有帮助",您对这种看法_____。

1）非常同意   2）同意

3）没有明确答案   4）不同意

5）坚决不同意

18. 对下面几类学生,您在纠错时会采用不同的方式吗?

外向学生↔内向学生_____

1）会   2）不会

如果会,表现在_____

_____。

男生↔女生_____

1）会   2）不会

如果会,表现在_____

_____。

英语水平高的学生↔英语水平低的学生_____

1）会   2）不会

如果会,表现在_____

_____。

非常有自信的学生↔缺乏自信的学生_____

1）会   2）不会

如果会,表现在_____

_____。

冒险性强的学生↔冒险性弱的学生_____

1）会   2）不会

如果会,表现在_____

_____。

发言时很紧张的学生↔发言时不紧张的学生_____

1）会   2）不会

如果会,表现在_____

_____。

147

二、请回答下列问题

1. 您认为纠正学生课堂发言中的错误有必要、有作用吗？为什么？

2. 您通常以怎样的态度对待学生口头表达中的错误？您的措辞是怎样的？

3. 您使用非语言方式帮助学生发现和改正发言中的错误吗？请详细说明。您觉得这种方式有效吗？

Appendix Ⅱ Questionnaire for students
问 卷 调 查

学校_____班级_____
姓名_____学号_____
性别_____年龄_____

这份问卷旨在了解同学们的基本情况以及英语学习方面的看法和做法,以改进教学。请务必根据你的实际情况如实填写。

请注意,问卷中提及的错误指**课堂对话**中的语言错误。

一、以下各项代表了某些想法和做法,并无好坏、对错之分。请根据每个数字所表达的意思,选择一个数字填在每句话后面的括号里。

> 1 = 这句话**完全**不适合我。
> 2 = 这句话**通常**不适合我。
> 3 = 这句话**有时**适合我。
> 4 = 这句话**通常**适合我。
> 5 = 这句话**完全**适合我。

1. 我相信自己的能力、潜力和价值。(   )
2. 我很多事情都做不好。(   )
3. 我常常让关心我的人失望。(   )
4. 我周围的大多数同学都比我强。(   )
5. 我喜欢用英语畅所欲言,并不特别在意语法方面的细节问题。(   )
6. 在英语课上发言时我充满自信。(   )
7. 在确切知道一个英语单词的用法前,我不会使用这个单词。(   )

8. 我不喜欢在课堂上尝试用英语表达复杂的想法。（　　　）

9. 上课发言时我担心同学笑话我。（　　　）

10. 对于老师的提问,我只有在确定自己的答案正确时,才主动发言。（　　　）

11. 在全班同学面前用英语发言让我感觉很不自在。（　　　）

12. 在口语表达中我不会使用没有把握的单词和句型。（　　　）

13. 上课发言时我会非常紧张。（　　　）

14. 我常常担心自己英语课跟不上。（　　　）

15. 即使我不完全确定一个词或句子是否完全适合于当前情况,我仍然会用它。（　　　）

16. 我害怕在英语课上发言。（　　　）

17. 我认为其他同学英语比我好。（　　　）

18. 说英语前我一般会先打腹稿再发言。（　　　）

19. 我认为纠正错误是必要的。（　　　）

20. 我平时很少注意到自己言语中的错误。（　　　）

21. 我认为纠正错误对学习有帮助。（　　　）

22. 我常常能意识到自己所犯的错误。（　　　）

23. 我认为错误不需要纠正。（　　　）

24. 很多言语中的错误我往往意识不到。（　　　）

25. 我认为纠正错误作用不大。（　　　）

26. 在老师或同学提醒后,我才意识到自己的错误。（　　　）

二、请在下列各题中选出一个适当选项,将答案写在横线上。

1. 我通常喜欢_____工作。

　　1）独自　　　　　　　　　　2）和大家一起

2. 我比较_____被人接近。

　　1）不容易　　　　　　　　　2）容易

3. 我最高兴的是_____。

　　1）与大家在一起　　　　　　2）不与别人在一起

4. 在聚会时,我_____。

　　1）只与熟人交谈　　　　　　2）喜欢与陌生人交谈

5. 在与别人的交往中,我通常_____。

1）不能及时得到别人的信息

2）能及时了解别人的近况

6. 如果我_____,通常能把事情做得更好。

1）与别人讨论

2）独自思考

7. 当与别人在一起时,我通常的特点是_____。

1）开朗、坦诚、愿意冒险

2）不愿跟别人谈自己的情况

8. 交朋友时,通常是_____主动。

1）别人   2）我

9. 我宁愿_____。

1）一个人呆在家里

2）参加没有多大兴趣的聚会

10. 和别人交往时,我总是_____。

1）兴致很高,觉得有很多话题要谈

2）尽量少说话

11. 与一群人在一起时,我通常_____。

1）等别人来找我讲话

2）主动找别人讲话

12. 当我一个人时,我感到_____。

1）清静   2）孤独

13. 在课堂上,我喜欢_____。

1）小组活动

2）独自进行某项活动

14. 当与别人发生争吵或辩论时,我喜欢_____。

1）把话说出来,希望当时当地就能得到解决

2）不讲话,希望问题能自行解决

15. 当我想把复杂的想法表达出来的时候,我通常感到_____。

1）非常艰难   2）比较容易

三、请回答下列问题：

1. 你很在意老师纠正你的错误时所采取的态度和措辞吗？你希望老师以怎样的态度和方式对待你的错误（请尽可能详细说明）？

2. 你认为所有的错误老师都应该纠正吗？你认为在什么情况下错误必须得到老师的纠正？为什么？

3. 老师采用的非语言方式（如表情、眼神、语调等）能帮助你发现或纠正错误吗？请说明是怎样的方式（请尽可能详细说明）。

四、请在下列各题中选出适当选项,没有特别说明的题目均为单选题。除了有具体要求的题目外,其余各题请将答案写在横线上。有些题目需加以说明,请在空格处填上你的想法。

1. 对于语言错误,我同意_____。

1)错误是失败的代名词,应尽量避免。

2)错误是语言学习过程中的重要组成部分,有积极作用。

2. 上课发言时我更注重_____。

1)语言形式　　　　　　　　2)表达内容

3. 我们在口语表达中常会出现几类错误,即语音错误、语法错误、词汇错误、表达错误(即看似正确却不符合英语表达习惯的错误)和语篇错误(即符合语法和表达习惯,但从上下文看让人无法理解的错误)。你认为哪类错误应首先得到纠正,哪类错误次之,请在你认为最有必要纠正的错误类型后的括号中填入1,次之的填2,依此类推,将1—5这几个数字填入括号。

语音错误(　　　)　　　　　　语法错误(　　　)

词汇错误(　　　)　　　　　　表达错误(　　　)

语篇错误(　　　)

4. 老师纠正的_____给我留下了最深刻的印象,我在以后使用英语时会注意改正。

1)语音错误　　　　　　　　2)语法错误

3)词汇错误　　　　　　　　4)表达错误

5)语篇错误

5. 在我们犯错时,有老师自己纠正的,也有老师让同学纠正的,还有老师让我们自己纠正的。我希望由_____来纠正我的错误(可单选或多选),我最希望由_____来纠正我的错误。

1)老师　　　　　　　　　　2)同学

3)自己

6. 对于发言中的错误,我希望老师_____。
   1)立即纠正　　　　　　　2)一句话说完后纠正
   3)表达结束时纠正　　　　4)上课时不纠正,课后纠正
   5)以后纠正

7. 当老师注意到我的错误并觉得有必要纠正时,通常情况下我希望老师_____。
   1)在课上纠正
   2)记下错误,以后和我单独交流
   3)记下错误,以后集中讲解和练习

8. 在课堂上我比较喜欢老师以这种方式纠错:_____(可选一到两项)。
   1)直接指出错误　　　　　2)直接说出正确用法
   3)给出提示,让我自己纠正

9. 对我来说最有效的纠错方式是_____。
   1)直接指出错误　　　　　2)直接说出正确用法
   3)给出提示,让我自己纠正

10. 老师在全班性课堂活动和小组讨论时可能会采用不同的方式纠错(比如在小组讨论时可能更直接)。你对此持什么观点?_____
    1)赞成　　　　　　　　　2)不赞成
    请说明原因:_____
    _____。

11. 两人活动或小组讨论时,我_____纠正同学语言表达中的错误,原因是_____
    _____。
    1)总是　　　　　　　　　2)经常
    3)有时　　　　　　　　　4)极少
    5)从不

12. 我通常纠正同学的_____(可单选或多选),纠正最多的是_____(可选一到两项)。
    1)语音错误　　　　　　　2)语法错误

3）词汇错误   4）表达错误

5）语篇错误

13. 纠正同学的错误时，我通常采用这样的方式：_____（可选一到两项）

 1）直接指出错误

 2）直接说出正确用法

 3）给出提示，让他（她）自己纠正

14. 我纠正同学的错误时，同学_____注意到。

 1）总是能   2）一般能

 3）有时能   4）极少能

 5）不能

15. 我喜欢同学以这样的方式纠正我的错误_____（可选一到两项）

 1）直接指出错误   2）直接说出正确用法

 3）给出提示，让我自己纠正

16. 对于同学纠正我的错误，我_____接受，原因是_____

_____。

 1）总是能   2）一般能

 3）有时能   4）极少能

 5）不能

17. 哪些同学纠正的错误你更能接受？请在每组答案中选一个：

 1）英语水平比我高   2）英语水平比我低

 3）英语水平和我差不多_____

 1）性格外向   2）性格内向

 3）外向和内向无所谓_____

 1）同性   2）异性

 3）同性或异性无所谓_____

 1）熟悉   2）不熟悉

 3）熟悉或不熟悉无所谓_____

 其他（选项中未包括的方面，请具体说明）_____

_____。

155

18. "同学纠错对英语学习有帮助",我对这种看法_____。

　　1）非常同意　　　　　　2）同意

　　3）没有明确答案　　　　4）不同意

　　5）坚决不同意

Appendix Ⅲ Interview questions for teachers

教师访谈问卷

1. 你觉得如何能提高语言水平和口语水平？你采用怎样的教学方法教学？

2. 第一题，"对于语言错误，我同意……，"为什么？错误的积极作用体现在哪里？您觉得学生有必要重视纠错吗？怎样使他们注意？

3. 第二题，"在课堂发言中，您的学生……意识到自己的语言错误"，哪些学生更易意识到自己的错误？

4. 第三题，"您在学生上课发言时更注重学生的……"，为什么？在给予反馈时您主要对什么做出评价，内容还是形式？通常您怎样说？

5. 第四题，"您在上课时……纠正学生的语言错误"，为什么？决定是否纠错时您通常会考虑到哪些问题？何时会纠正？何时不会纠正？

6. 第五题，"您的学生在课堂发言中最常出现的是……"，学生常犯的语音错误有哪些？语法错误、词汇错误、表达错误、语篇错误呢？

7. 第七题，您为什么这样给这些错误排序呢？

8. 第八题，您为什么这样排序呢？

9. 第十一题，"课堂纠错时，您采用以下方式纠错的频率是……"，为什么？

10. 您最常采用的是什么纠错方式？具体怎么纠？后四种方法，学生通常怎么反应？他们有反馈吗？哪种方式最有效？学生通常能自己纠正错误吗？哪些学生不能纠正？如果纠正了还有错误怎么办？

11. 每种纠错方式中针对的学生有所不同吗（水平，性格，性别，

157

自信心,对语言水平的自信心,语言焦虑感,对错误的意识程度)? 哪些学生较多?

12. 在纠错时,您通过什么知道学生注意到了您的否定反馈? 哪些学生更易注意到你的反馈呢?

13. 第十二题,"对于学生课堂发言中出现各类错误您是否采用不同方式纠错? ……",为什么? 每种错误如何纠正您能举例说明吗?

14. 第十四题,"您通常在这样的情况下让学生自己纠正错误,……",为什么?

Appendix Ⅳ Interview questions for students
学生访谈问卷

1. 你觉得我们应该怎么学好一门语言？平时学习时你是否会注意词汇、语法规则的学习，还是注重培养语感？你希望达到怎样的语言水平？

2. 你在课堂上积极发言吗？你在发言时有紧张的感觉吗？怎么紧张？为什么？什么情况下、老师怎样做会让你紧张？你喜欢怎样的课堂氛围？什么样的老师让你感觉在课堂上发言比较放松、更放得开？

3. 就外语学习者来说，在发言时常会出现错误。你怎么看待错误？害怕犯错吗？新学的东西你会用吗？

4. 你在口语表达中最大的问题是什么？犯错频率很高吗？错误很多吗？你在口语表达中出现的语音错误主要是什么方面的？能举例吗？其它的错误呢？

5. 第四题，"老师纠正的……给你留下了最深刻的印象，"为什么？你觉得口语中所有的错误都该纠正吗？哪些该纠正？

6. 发言中自己的错误你能意识到吗？有没有错误老师和同学发现后指出来？有多少？马上纠正的频率高吗？发言后会想想吗？当你意识到自己表达中有错会怎么想？

7. 第二题，"课堂发言时更注重……"，为什么？

8. 第三题，"你认为最需要纠正的是……"，为什么这么排序？

9. 第五题，"希望由……来纠正我的错误，最希望由……纠正"，为什么？课堂上老师让别的同学纠错，你怎么想？

10. 你注意老师的反馈吗？发言时老师会有反馈吗？内容还是形式？你希望老师更注重内容还是形式反馈？老师怎样纠错？直接纠错，重述，提示让你自纠，哪个频率更高？感觉？什么情况下你能意识到老师在纠错？

11. 第八题和第九题,"你希望老师以……方式纠错,最有效的方式是……",为什么?

12. 第六题,"你希望老师……纠错",为什么?

13. 第七题,"当老师认为错误有必要纠正时,希望老师……纠正",为什么?

14. 老师的眼神、表情和语调对你的发言有影响吗?怎样的方式能帮助你发现错误?(问答题3)你希望老师在纠正你的错误时怎么做?

15. 第十题,"老师全班活动和小组采用不同纠错方式,你……",为什么?

16. 小组讨论时你注意听同学的发言吗?你注意内容还是形式?你能经常注意到同学发言中的错误吗?

17. 第十二题,"小组讨论时我通常纠正同学的……错误",为什么?

18. 第十三题,"你通常采用……方式纠正同学的错误",为什么?

19. 第十四题,"我纠正同学的错误时,同学……注意到",同学没有注意到你纠正错误,你怎么办?有没有同学不能接受你的做法?哪些同学?

20. 第十五题,"你喜欢同学以……方式纠错",为什么?

21. 第十六题,"同学指出的错误,你……接受",为什么?

22. 第十七题,"……同学纠错你更能接受",为什么?